Lost & Found

Lost & Found

Reflections on Travel, Career, Love and Family

Dustin Grinnell

PETER LANG
Oxford · Berlin · Bruxelles · Chennai · Lausanne · New York

Bibliographic information published by the Deutsche Nationalbibliothek. The German National Library lists this publication in the German National Bibliography; detailed bibliographic data is available on the Internet at http://dnb.d-nb.de.

A catalogue record for this book is available from the British Library.

Library of Congress Cataloging-in-Publication Data

Names: Grinnell, Dustin, 1983- author.
Title: Lost & found : reflections on travel, career, love and family / Dustin Grinnell.
Other titles: Lost and found
Description: Oxford ; New York : Peter Lang, 2024.
Identifiers: LCCN 2023047489 (print) | LCCN 2023047490 (ebook) | ISBN 9781803741840 (paperback) | ISBN 9781803741857 (ebook) | ISBN 9781803741864 (epub)
Subjects: LCSH: Grinnell, Dustin, 1983- | Authors, American—21st century—Biography. | LCGFT: Autobiographies. | Essays.
Classification: LCC PS3607.R568246 Z46 2024 (print) | LCC PS3607.R568246 (ebook) | DDC 814/.6 [B]—dc23/eng/20231017
LC record available at https://lccn.loc.gov/2023047489
LC ebook record available at https://lccn.loc.gov/2023047490

Cover image: "Mist and Cloud Surrounding The Forest", photograph by Emily Norton, iStock <https://www.istockphoto.com/portfolio/EmilyNorton>.
Cover design by Peter Lang Group AG

ISBN 978-1-80374-184-0 (print)
ISBN 978-1-80374-185-7 (ePDF)
ISBN 978-1-80374-186-4 (ePub)
DOI 10.3726/b21471

© 2024 Peter Lang Group AG, Lausanne
Published by Peter Lang Ltd, Oxford, United Kingdom
info@peterlang.com - www.peterlang.com

Dustin Grinnell has asserted his right under the Copyright, Designs and Patents Act, 1988, to be identified as Author of this Work.

All rights reserved.
All parts of this publication are protected by copyright.
Any utilisation outside the strict limits of the copyright law, without the permission of the publisher, is forbidden and liable to prosecution.
This applies in particular to reproductions, translations, microfilming, and storage and processing in electronic retrieval systems.

This publication has been peer reviewed.

Man is condemned to be free; because once thrown into the world, he is responsible for everything he does. It is up to you to give [life] meaning.
—Jean-Paul Sartre

Contents

Preface — xi

Acknowledgments — xv

Introduction — 1

PART I Lost — 7

CHAPTER 1
A Sudden Stab of Murky Suspicion — 9

CHAPTER 2
Up Fever Slope — 13

CHAPTER 3
The Dizziness of Freedom — 17

CHAPTER 4
A Taste of Glory — 27

CHAPTER 5
A Lesson in Safety — 31

CHAPTER 6
Missing Paris — 35

CHAPTER 7
The Hate Game   41

CHAPTER 8
Departing Down the Middle   53

PART II   Departed   55

CHAPTER 9
In Defense of Quixote   57

CHAPTER 10
Finding My Sleep in China   65

CHAPTER 11
Backed up in China   73

CHAPTER 12
Walkabout Love   77

CHAPTER 13
Letters from Dad   83

CHAPTER 14
Hoedown at McDonald's   91

CHAPTER 15
Doubt Isn't Sexy   95

Contents

CHAPTER 16
Keeping the Channel Open — 97

CHAPTER 17
Fake It 'til You Make It — 101

PART III   Found — 107

CHAPTER 18
The Gift of Pain — 109

CHAPTER 19
A Morning Dose of Awe — 131

CHAPTER 20
The Stick — 133

CHAPTER 21
How to Fix a Bluey Heart — 137

CHAPTER 22
Corporate Disobedience — 145

CHAPTER 23
Forest Medicine — 165

CHAPTER 24
The Language of My Father — 167

CHAPTER 25
Learning to Love My Fate   171

Epilogue   179

Publication History   183

Preface

It's always been my natural inclination to make sense of myself and the world through writing. The process of writing nonfiction and fiction has offered a way to examine my inner life, a method for exploring ideas that have captured my imagination, a means for understanding the human condition, and a way to discover the truth. Fundamentally, writing has allowed me to ask important questions. Who am I? What do I want? How should I live?

While experimenting with different genres—including travel and science writing, memoir, literary journalism, and fiction—I fell in love with the personal essay a decade ago. The verb *essay* means to try or attempt. Likewise, the personal essay genre allows writers to contemplate, experiment, and discover. It's an exhilarating, versatile genre that provides a space for writers to interrogate the world and reflect on themselves. Through personal essays, I have arrived at insights about myself and my life that have led to a better understanding of why certain events might have happened. I have been able to make sense of childhood traumas and reframe painful events into personally meaningful stories. In doing so, I have loosened the grip these events hold on my psyche.

According to sociological research, people are better at coping with difficult circumstances if they can explain how and why they occurred. In the 1990s, American psychologist James Pennebaker revealed this through a study on the effects of expressive writing. Volunteers who had experienced traumatic events were asked to journal about their painful experiences for fifteen to twenty minutes a day for four days.

A year later, Pennebaker compared their health records with the records of the volunteers in the control group, each of whom had experienced a traumatic event but hadn't written it down. The results showed that those who wrote about their experiences had fewer health issues than those who didn't. Likewise, many issues in our lives become endurable once we know what they represent. As psychologist Carl Jung noted, neurotic symptoms are "the suffering of a soul which has not discovered its meaning."

The twenty-five essays in *Lost & Found* are my attempts to make sense of my life and find meaning in my experiences. Written over ten years, these stories represent my journey from losing myself in my twenties to finding myself in my thirties. The book is broken up into three parts: "Lost," "Departed," and "Found."

In Part I, the essay, "A Sudden Stab of Murky Suspicion," explores how knowing when to trust my intuition can be difficult, especially in a foreign land. "Up Fever Slope" captures my trek up Mount Kilimanjaro in my mid-twenties and touches on how I sometimes ignored messages from reality, like altitude sickness. "The Dizziness of Freedom" covers my travels in New Zealand and narrates the birth of bungee jumping. In it, I explore the notion of "the dizziness of freedom," a phrase coined by the nineteenth-century Danish philosopher Søren Kierkegaard that refers to the anxiety that can arise when we're overcome by too many choices.

The next essay, "A Taste of Glory," explores my running of the Newport Marathon, in which I was determined to break the four-hour mark, a demonstration of my perpetual need to manufacture a goal worth striving for. Likewise, in "Missing Paris," I wrote about being so absorbed in the goal to break the four-hour mark at the Paris Marathon, I almost missed the chance to admire the city. Meanwhile, "A Lesson in Safety" is about living a safe city life and realizing that a fully risk-averse existence presents its own danger. To combat this, I placed myself in a risky situation by riding my motorcycle from Cambridge, MA, to Walden Pond the day I learned how to ride it.

In "The Hate Game," I examine the disintegration of a relationship and provide an interpretation of my first encounter with psychotherapy, where I began to confront myself—my early life, in particular. In the final essay in Part I, "Departing Down the Middle," I wrote about dropping my girlfriend off at the airport before she moved to the West Coast. The essay evokes Buddhism to take the sting out of the event, but this spiritual theory denies the pain of a failing relationship.

Part II, "Departed," captures the beginning of my search for more meaning in my life. I was 33 years old and needed time for exploration,

Preface

so I submitted an application for a Fulbright–National Geographic Storytelling Fellowship. When it didn't make the cut, I decided to quit my job and carry out the proposal on my own by traveling to China to learn about the country's traditional medicine. "Finding My Sleep in China" and "Backed Up in China" are about arriving at my host institution in Beijing to learn about Chinese medicine. After leaving the city, I traveled another three thousand miles through the enormous country. I intended to travel alone, still grieving my failed relationship, until I met a young Chinese woman while waiting to take a boat down the Li River. "Walkabout Love" discusses how enjoyable it was to make a genuine connection so far from home.

Three weeks later, I was stateside at my father's house in Eaton, NH. "Letters from Dad" covers the six weeks I spent there, coming to terms with losses in my youth—in particular, the death of my grandmother when I was seventeen. The essay was inspired by my father, whose favorite axiom encouraged the cross-country journey I set out on next: "Geologically speaking, a human life is only ten seconds long." After several weeks of preparation, I took off on a thirty-day, 4,300-mile road trip on my motorcycle. The essay "In Defense of Quixote" tries to capture my ambivalence over ditching my job to go on a modern-day pilgrimage. While it felt inspiring to take a year off and commit to writing full-time, I also wondered if it was a mistake.

Part III, "Found," begins with "The Gift of Pain." I had returned from my journey with various psychosomatic maladies that doctors couldn't explain. A quest to uncover the causes with doctors led me into the depths of my psychology, where I learned that sadness and anger have infinitely creative ways of seeking attention. The essay is about how I healed my physical problems by addressing emotional pain.

The essays in Part III concern my constant search for identity. "A Morning Dose of Awe" examines how the TV show *Sunrise Earth* gave me a much-needed break from the morning news. "The Language of My Father" is a humorous look at my father's written communication style. "The Stick" explores how I worked to replace an idealized version of my father with a more realistic view of him. "How to Fix a Bluey Heart" explores my interactions with a woman who helped me get over a previous relationship and taught me how to love again. "Corporate Disobedience" delves into my attempt to find a new way of seeing myself in the workplace, as someone who challenges and resists illegitimate authorities. And "Forest Medicine" covers a walk I took in the forest as a respite from the stresses of living in the city. "Learning to Love My Fate," the last essay, works through my struggle to come to terms with outgrowing my decade of writing marketing content for business. It also includes the realization that having a day job supports my creative life and the fact that perhaps I already have everything I need.

In my view, the essays of *Lost & Found* represent an end of the beginning. My current 40-year-old self who finished this book is a bit more aware, a little more mature, and a tad wiser than my 30-year-old self who started it. Call it coming of age, growth, or maturity. But I'll never be truly "found," in my opinion. I'll always cycle through stages of losing myself and finding myself. I'll always be called to shed my skin and reinvent myself throughout life. And answering these calls to change is the tough work of living.

My purpose in creating this collection was to write sincerely about what I've thought and felt in my four decades on this planet. In doing so, I hope others might relate to some of my experiences and perhaps gain insight into their lives or learn something about themselves in the process. By writing about my experiences and describing them in these essays, I also exert some control over the events I explore, which I believe helps liberate me from them. Writing these personal essays was a freedom-making process: freedom from my past, freedom from my present, and the freedom to always make new choices to start my life anew.

Acknowledgments

I'm grateful for the talented editors I've worked with over the years. As always, I'd like to thank Tod Tinker, who provides thorough editing and fact-checking and helps make my stories clearer and more coherent. Thank you to my father, Greg Grinnell, for urging me to never stop dreaming. Thanks to Sam Cooke for supporting me no matter what I decide to do.

Finally, I'd like to thank my former therapist, John Grillo, who helped me look deeper inside myself, explore further, and better understand myself. On our many journeys into the past and speculations about the future, we churned up previously unconscious material and fashioned it into a coherent narrative, thereby allowing me to have control over much that had been out of my conscious awareness. Over time, I became less of a stranger to myself—going from lost to found.

Introduction

In 2008, I enrolled in a Ph.D. program at Penn State University to study physiology, the science of how the human body works. I've always been fascinated with the subject, from how the heart beats to how the brain perceives, and I excelled at it in college. Despite my passion for science, though, I knew the program was the wrong fit for me within the first few months of enrollment. I had worked in a small biotechnology lab after college and had found the work interesting, but an academic lab turned out to be unstimulating. The questions were too limited, and I couldn't see myself teaching at a university or leading a lab at a school or company.

To be honest, I went to grad school only after failing the entrance exam for medical school. When the path I had spent over a decade preparing for was no longer available, I applied to doctoral programs to tidy up my next few years. Yet nine months into the Ph.D. program, I transferred to a master's program in physiology. I wasn't going to spend the next five years in grad school, so my future was again open to possibilities. I wanted to leverage my science degree to do something that better suited my personality and skills, so I read a book about alternative careers in science. A chapter on science writing jumped out at me. I had a passion for writing and was fascinated by many areas of science, though mostly at the theoretical rather than the practical level. As I closed the book, I knew I didn't want to "do" science. Instead, I would write about it.

While completing the requirements of my master's degree, I sought an internship with my university's research publications office. The editor took a chance on me, and I began interviewing scientists and writing newspaper-style science articles for the school paper. It was exciting to talk with experts in fields like entomology, materials science, and computer science and tackle the challenge of popularizing their research for general readers. By the time I graduated a year later, I knew I wanted to become a writer.

After earning my degree, I returned to Boston and applied for writing jobs. I didn't want to work as a reporter at a newspaper or magazine, though. I was adamant about finding a position as a copywriter. The work seemed dynamic, creatively demanding, and even enjoyable. Eventually, I landed a copywriting position at a research company and cut my teeth on everything related to commercial writing, from brochures to videos, from articles to advertisements.

For the next ten years, I worked similar jobs at Boston-based research companies, nonprofits, a major hospital, and a technology company. These were rough-and-tumble years, as I learned the business of turning science and medicine into persuasive content. At the same time, I was also writing fiction. I wrote three science fiction novels, cautionary tales of technology written in the style of a literary hero, Michael Crichton, author of *Jurassic Park*. I also published several short stories in literary journals. Eventually, I collected thirteen of my short stories into *The Healing Book*, a collection of stories about self-discovery and healing.

Between jobs and during two-week vacations, I traveled the world in search of adventure. I bungee jumped in New Zealand and ran the Paris marathon. I watched a sunrise from the top of Mount Kilimanjaro and rode my motorcycle across the United States, from New Hampshire to Southern California. Yet, in all my travels, I seldom looked inward. In my desire for new experiences, I didn't understand what I was striving for or what my real feelings were. I was a stranger to myself.

It wasn't until I began psychotherapy in my early thirties that I began to use my adventurous spirit to explore my mind and heart. With a kind, inquisitive social worker as my guide, I peered into my childhood, unearthed painful memories, and discovered a more authentic, less restless self. My path to psychotherapy began in Cambridge, MA, where I wrote about science at a biomedical research institute. I enjoyed the work, but I felt cooped up in the city and disenchanted with office life. I had self-published two novels and had published many pieces of nonfiction. After several years of corporate work, I was itching to move on.

At the time, I was trying my hand at screenwriting. I wrote a feature-length screenplay that mirrored my time working as a corporate writer on the executive floor of a major research company. It earned second place in a contest and received an encouraging review from a director in Los Angeles. I had been a movie buff since I was a kid, and people were now telling me I might be good at writing screenplays. I began to wonder whether I should commit to writing movies. Maybe I could make a go of writing on my own, I thought. If I didn't leap in my thirties, I might never do it.

I decided to quit my job and embark on a pilgrimage, a time to reflect on my life. My year-long journey would have three acts: First, I would backpack through China for three weeks to study traditional Chinese medicine, a journey I decided to undertake despite my proposal not being accepted for a Fulbright–National Geographic Storytelling Fellowship. Second, I would spend six weeks with my father in my hometown in the White Mountains of New Hampshire. Third, I would drive my 1982 Honda Nighthawk across the country to California to break into screenwriting.

The decision felt radical, perhaps akin to a midlife crisis. It was a time of great transition for me, and the commitment to quit my job and move to California to break into the competitive industry of screenwriting filled me with uncertainty and fear. Was I inspired or delusional? As I planned my travels, I read *Don Quixote* by Miguel de Cervantes and wrote an essay that examined my doubts through the lens of the novel. The piece explored—*defended*—Don Quixote's ability to delude himself into believing anything through magical thinking. Quixote could falsify reality to be convinced of any truth. I, too, had this capacity for reality distortion. The skill could lead to self-determination and had fueled various achievements in my life. But sometimes, it could also lead me into self-delusion.

A year into my California dream, I had yet to land a screenwriting assignment, and my body rebelled. I developed chronic lower back pain and mysterious neurological symptoms, including aching joints and tingling limbs. For the first time in my life, I experienced anxiety, and two panic attacks landed me in the emergency room. Even after leaving the hospital, the panic was a constant, unwelcome companion. I didn't recognize it then, but my body and brain were sending me messages that I was living a lie.

Knowing I was unwell, I decided to return to Boston to recover. I got a job as a writer for a hospital and enrolled in a master of fine arts (MFA) program for fiction writing, and my life returned to how it had been before.

With the return of stability and financial security and the help of good doctors and a therapist I trusted, I recovered.

In time, I reflected on my failure. As I had suspected in my essay about *Don Quixote*, I had been out of touch with reality. Like Quixote, I had been tilting at windmills. Had I seen Quixote's fantasies as a cautionary tale, I might've prevented my misfortune. Yet I had seen reality the way I wanted and paid a high price.

Friends and family were pleased to see me back on my feet, but they were troubled by the detail in which I wanted to unpack my struggles in California. They told me to move on and live my life, but I wanted to understand why things had happened the way they had. So, with the help of my insightful and humorous therapist, I attempted to make sense of why I had stumbled. Together, we arranged the events around my fall into a coherent narrative with a beginning, middle, and end.

As I began to recognize why I had made certain choices and why particular events had occurred, my body and mind began to settle. The lower back pain subsided, and the anxiety and depressive symptoms lifted. I started to realize that when I set off on my pilgrimage, I had been running full tilt at my dreams, looking for excitement and adventure and trying to live an "authentic" life. However, I had been puffed up with hubris, and my goals had been unrealistic. I had deluded myself.

A year into working with my therapist, I asked him what he'd say to a colleague who asked what my "problems" were. Given that my physical symptoms were clearly manifestations of unprocessed emotional or psychological troubles, he had diagnosed somatic symptom disorder, or psychosomatic illness. However, he believed my main issues had to do with matters of identity. "I would tell my colleague," he said, "Dustin needs to figure out who he is and what he wants."

With this feedback, I looked at my life through the lens of a self-concept issue. In terms of career, I enjoyed the excitement of writing creatively for businesses, but I felt I had outgrown my role as a hired gun. I had started to admire "real" writers: novelists, journalists, and essayists who explored the truth and wrote about things that mattered. As my discontent over writing marketing material for businesses grew, I often referred to myself as a corporate hack or a propagandist among friends and even colleagues.

At the same time, I was coming to terms with the fact that I didn't fit into hierarchical corporate environments. I began to see them as dictatorships, sometimes populated by authorities who were illegitimate due to their lack of skill, untrustworthiness, or lack of purpose other than to maintain existing power structures. More and more, I was compelled to question and challenge the illegitimate authorities I encountered in office settings.

Even now, my therapist's words ring in my ears, and I continue to ask of myself: Who am I, and what do I want? While I have perhaps grown out of my role as a writer for businesses, I haven't figured out what to do next. There's still a disconnect between who I am and who I think I can be as a writer. It's the dream of any writer to be able to write what we want, when we want, without having to worry about money. While I have had some publishing success with my writing, I haven't yet figured out how to make a living from my creative work. Even now, I work to close the gap between my present self and the idealized self I hope to become.

In this respect, I remind myself that I won't ever "arrive." No relationship and no amount of money, status, or power will bring me the life I think I desire. Chasing such things is to pursue an illusion and could be the path to despair. Indeed, even when I get what I want, I acclimate to a set of new problems. I now know that my life will never be free of struggle. With this in mind, I still aim to engage in the process of life, commit to a meaningful purpose, and structure my life around intrinsically satisfying activities. For me, I will continue writing as a way to make sense of what it means to be alive.

PART I

Lost

2014–2016

People say that what we're all seeking is a meaning for life. I don't think that's what we're really seeking. I think that what we're seeking is an experience of being alive.

—Joseph Campbell

CHAPTER 1

A Sudden Stab of Murky Suspicion

It wasn't our guide who made me suspicious; it was the bystander, a short woman in a vibrant dress with bananas in her hand.

Our guide had been confident during our tour of Arusha, Tanzania, not the least bit shady. "This way," he said, "Right through here," as he pointed to a shoddy door on the side of a nondescript building.

The woman, however, was shifty, her eyes twitching, her too-still body poised, begging, "Don't go, you fools, it's a trap."

"Wait," I said, motionless.

My friend, John, stopped and turned, followed by the guide, who looked confused.

The half-day adventure through the busy town in northern Tanzania, which served as a jumping-off point for safaris and treks up Mount Kilimanjaro, had been fun and stimulating, but most importantly, and often surprisingly, it had been safe. And the guide, a scrawny twenty-something from a neighboring town, had been accommodating and seemed genuine, despite his obvious desire for us to buy one of his paintings at the tour's conclusion.

But as the woman beside him shuffled her feet anxiously, I began to reconfigure my impression of the young man. The sudden hint of danger had cast the local artisan in a different, less-than-hospitable light. In return for a few swirls of paint, a quid pro quo I was certain he performed regularly, perhaps he had wanted more than a few of our American dollars.

The woman hadn't nodded at me, she hadn't slipped me a note, and she hadn't screamed, "Run!" But I had reacted, nonetheless. She had given something away, exposed our guide somehow.

"No," I said, despite the fact no one had addressed my hesitancy.

"But this is last part of the tour," the guide responded eagerly, placing his palm on John's backpack. Suddenly, I began a game of connect-the-dots.

Like breadcrumbs, I followed the details of the last few hours back to the moment when our guide discovered us at our hostel's front door, wading through a crowd of peddlers and beggars, offering us refuge in a cozy alleyway where he stashed his artwork for purchase.

"I can show you around Arusha," he had prodded.

We told him no a handful of times but ultimately, adventurously, agreed.

His services required such persistence, I thought, but not taking no for an answer should have been our first tipoff. The second had been his speech; it was choppy and quick, like a coffeehouse barista who'd done too much of her own stuff. And the guide had loved John's Gore-Tex boots, joking with a grin that he could leave them with him before we returned to Boston.

His quip had seemed benign then, but now, my eyes glued to the nervous woman, the remark seemed like a canned observation likely bestowed upon countless wide-eyed tourists who came before us, and before them.

"Take us back to our hostel, please," I said, now convinced that the "last leg" of our tour was a trap and that hiding inside the building was a gang of thieves, their duffel bags stuffed with the wallets, watches, and purses of unsuspecting tourists.

The guide's face dropped, his head shifting backward. Saying nothing, he pivoted and dodged the building on our way back to the center of town. Was he disappointed that his plan, which had likely worked without a hitch countless times before, had been foiled? Or was he insulted by my silent accusation, a subtextual jab that he was a fraud, a criminal even?

If we had entered that building, would we have come upon danger or wonder, thieves with machetes, or an oasis, brimming with sensory treasures? I'll never know.

Intuition is funny like that. It deals in subtleties, rascally details subject to perception, environment, biases, and false cues from objects and especially humans, like an onlooker who had put my nerves in overdrive. Had I misread the situation? The woman could have just heard a terrible bit of news, after all. She could have been searching desperately for a missing child.

Maybe, humiliatingly, she had found *our* presence unnerving.

As we walked back to our hostel, I felt a slight embarrassment, wondering if perhaps I had overreacted, if maybe I had been victim to my heightened senses, my own prejudices and fears, provoked by a lowdown building in a foreign country at the edge of an unfamiliar town. But I also felt grateful that I had followed my instincts, thankful that I had let the woman on the periphery inform my senses. Right or wrong, appropriate or obnoxious, clever or foolish, I had listened to the tiny details only my intuition had noticed and knew that was the best I, or anybody for that matter, could do.

CHAPTER 2

Up Fever Slope

Hours before our attempt to summit Mount Kilimanjaro in Tanzania, I slid into a sleeping bag in our hut at 15,000 feet and tried to sleep. In what seemed like minutes, I awoke out of breath, gasping. In the bunk bed below, my friend, John, slept soundly. He described himself as a couch potato. I'd recently run a marathon. Yet, John was the one comfortable at altitude while my head felt like it was pinned between the pavement and the wheel of a semi-trailer. It was the most wicked of hangovers without a remedy.

Even before I bought a plane ticket to East Africa, I knew I was susceptible to altitude sickness. A trip to Colorado years ago made that painfully clear. Yet I had journeyed to Tanzania with visions of a summit sunrise on Africa's highest peak. I convinced myself I'd be fine. Now, trying to sleep before our attempt to summit, my body was telling me just how delusional I'd been. Ambition had blinded me to the truth. I was vulnerable, and there was no way to avoid it.

At midnight, our guide woke us from a restless slumber, and porters prepared food. We were urged to eat, but the thought was as appealing as downing a candy bar after a pint of ice cream. I strapped a headlamp to my forehead and gazed up at the last trail we'd ascend, a series of switchbacks culminating at the peak, nearly 20,000 feet above the savannah of Tanzania.

As I clicked on my lamp, I searched my past for precedents of uncommon endurance and courage, hoping the memories of football games, rugby matches, triathlons, and marathons might steel my resolve and help me overcome the inevitable pain. But no memory snapped me out of my oxygen-deprived stupor. Our trekking guide beckoned us to the trailhead, and I knew nothing but turning back would unscrew the vise squeezing my brain. In such rarefied air, illusions seemed to provide little immunity. My headache would persist, most likely worsen.

On the border of Kenya and Tanzania, Mount Kilimanjaro rises to 19,340 majestic feet. We had climbed the Marangu route, the least technical trail up "Kili," which featured stops over six days at huts with bunk beds, sponge mattresses and pillows. The first day of our climb began in the rainforest at the Marangu gate at 6,046 feet. That morning, we hiked through high grasslands and sprawling vegetation and then slept at Mandara hut at 8,858 feet. The second day we trekked to Horombo hut at 12,205 feet. Higher altitude, thinner air. With the decreased air pressure, less oxygen enters your lungs and, therefore, your bloodstream.

I wasn't in any noticeable pain at 10,000 feet—the altitude where symptoms of Acute Mountain Sickness (AMS) typically emerge—but I was breathing faster and more heavily. To adjust to the thin air, our guide had built an acclimatization day into our itinerary, which included ascending to the Mawenzi hut at 14,160 feet, where we spent half a day relaxing, and then returning to Horombo hut for the night. It's a classic trick mountaineers have used for centuries. "Climb high, sleep low," means you reach a maximum altitude and then return to a lower height to sleep. The jolt stimulates short-term physiological adaptations, such as an increase in respiration as well as a faster and more forcefully pumping heart. However, six days at high altitude doesn't allow for long-term adaptations, a process that can take weeks.

On the fourth day, we left Horombo hut and headed to Kibo hut. It was the last stop before the summit. At this point, I was a prisoner to the altitude, the thin air a constant reminder that I was a stranger in a strange land. I had no appetite. I was always thirsty. I felt light-headed, dog-tired, and dizzy. Ibuprofen didn't put a dent in the headache, and lying down only made the situation worse. I dry-heaved often, and always felt on the verge of vomiting. Terrain on which I could navigate easily at sea level became a perilous tightrope walk at high altitude.

Of course, we had taken precautions. John and I ate a diet high in carbohydrates, which is known to enhance altitude tolerance. We even took a prescription drug called acetazolamide to prevent acute mountain sickness. But it had no effect other than to make my toes and fingers tingle.

At the last hut on Kilimanjaro, we weren't in the infamous "Death Zone"—the point at 25,000 feet upon which your body begins to consume itself to produce energy—it was more like the bend-your-arm-behind-your-back-and-say-uncle zone. With altitude sickness, fluid begins to accumulate in the lungs, a condition known as pulmonary edema. A far graver condition can follow called cerebral edema, which can induce a coma and death. The only treatment is to descend.

Before we left for Uhuru Peak, I asked our guide why we were leaving at midnight. He said it was best we not be able to see what we were climbing. Indeed, even from our limited point of view, the trail, composed of gray ash and loose stones, looked nightmarish. With each arduous step forward, I slid back two. Longing for comfort, for oxygen, I wished time away. I tried mental tricks. I dreamed of cold beers and Sunday football. I counted my steps, dedicated strides to friends and family. None of them helped. Behind me, John occasionally braced me as I lost my footing and staggered.

As we trudged upward through the frigid air, we passed other hikers also stricken by altitude sickness. The scenes were apocalyptic, people dry-heaving and holding their heads in their hands. They looked the way a fish does when tossed onto the floor of a boat—stunned, breathless, ready to die. I recalled the first stories of altitude sickness in the text, "Ch'ien Han Shu," a historical account of China from 206 BC to AD 25. "Again on passing the Great Headache Mountain, the Little Headache Mountain, and the Red Land and the Fever Slope, men's bodies become feverish, they lose color and are attacked with headaches and vomiting," was how early climbers described the route between China and Afghanistan.

After six agonizing hours, we reached the rim of Uhuru's crater. As if by voodoo magic, the sun poked through the clouds. Radiant streaks of red and orange glistened off toothed glaciers, warming the air and climbers' hearts. I was relieved to be standing at Africa's highest point, my eyes resting on milky clouds. I found myself teary-eyed and introspective, wondering about my decision to climb the big mountain. I knew I likely would suffer. I came anyway. I felt relieved that I hadn't hurt myself. Our guide had noticed the symptoms of altitude sickness; it was written all over my face. Twice he had asked me if I wanted to turn back, and twice I had rejected the notion.

We still had to descend, the most dangerous part of climbing any mountain. We took a different route down than the hellish route up, and it proved heavenly. The first section of the trail was a long slope of warm sand and rock fragments, which I sprinted through, sloshing my legs. Breathing came more freely.

The adventure made me realize that achievers can be a peculiar, sometimes dishonest bunch, mostly to themselves. Not admitting one's vulnerabilities can be a strength. Perhaps a foolish one, but a strength, nonetheless. It allows us to transform ourselves, to move beyond our perceived boundaries.

Mountains expose our self-deceptions and therefore help us face reality when we have willfully suppressed it. Rather than banish truth, they force us to see it, embrace it, and make peace with it.

Because no matter how hard we try, the truth eventually makes itself known.

CHAPTER 3

The Dizziness of Freedom

AJ Hackett cased the Eiffel Tower for over a month. He studied architectural plans and knew the guards' schedules. He memorized the exits, knew when the lights switched on and off. He and his team rehearsed radio dialogue that would intentionally distract security. During a reconnaissance visit, AJ determined the exact distance from the tower's second level to the ground by tying a stone to the end of a nylon cord and tossing it off the side.

The night before AJ bungee jumped down the center of the Eiffel Tower, he and his team entered it at 10 p.m., an hour before closing. Everyone had a role in the stunt, especially the cameraman, responsible for securing the sport's place in history. They paid their entry fees and entered separately, so as to avoid detection. Their backpacks were stuffed with rope, bungee cords, carabiners, camera gear, harnesses, and sleeping bags. And a bottle of champagne.

"Looking around the faces of the team, I saw a mixture of nervousness and excitement," AJ wrote in his autobiography, *Jump Start*. "We were enthusiastic amateurs playing some sort of warped espionage game." He and his team reached the bar on the second level and enjoyed a beer before close. They gulped down the last of their drinks, synchronized their watches, and split up. While AJ and two others scaled a fence and climbed toward a roof where they would sleep for the night, others distracted guards with idle chatter or blocked cameras with umbrellas or sheets of cardboard. AJ's girlfriend, Caroline, and her friend, Sara, played the role of "eye candy" in the security room, where they preoccupied the guards.

Then a security guard strolled dangerously close to the operation. The team pretended to be tourists, and after a few minutes, the guard passed. The support team exited the tower and congregated at the base, prepared to sleep outside. Just as AJ settled into sleep, an argument erupted: his cameraman was having second thoughts. Apparently, the man had just made a film in the Middle East, and his nerves hadn't recovered. AJ helped him over a fence. "It was a hiccup," he said, "but not a disaster. We still had two photographers on the tower and a cameraman shooting from various points on the ground." So, he tucked himself into his sleeping bag and fell asleep within minutes.

***

AJ Hackett's first bungee jump was in 1986 off of the Greenhithe Bridge in Auckland, New Zealand. His friend Chris Sigglekow introduced him to the idea. In the 1970s, Chris witnessed students from Oxford University's Dangerous Sports Club jump off a bridge in Bristol, England, with a rubber cord tied to their feet. He tried it himself a few years later, bungee jumping off the thirty-three-foot Pelorous Bridge near Nelson, New Zealand, using the same parachute cord he and AJ used for the Greenhithe Bridge.

AJ and Chris had discussed the cord's strength and stretch capacity before the jump, as well as the harness, knots, and ties. They purchased a parachute harness from a yachting store in Auckland and created a rigging system with climbing gear. They met with researchers at the University of Auckland to understand how long and thick a cord must be in order to be safe. They were told that a strand of rubber cord will break at 6.7 times its length when stretched out. At four times its length, it would be at 15 percent its breaking strain. "That gave us a massive safety margin," AJ wrote. To calculate the length of the cord before a jump, they divided the height by four. To account for different weights, they simply adjusted the thickness.

After measuring the height of Greenhithe Bridge, AJ and Chris strapped diving belts to a punching bag and tossed it off the side. They made sure the bags matched their body weights. After watching video footage of the tests, they were sure the concept was sound. "When it came time for us to jump ourselves," AJ said, "we had no fear at all." He called the sixty-two-foot bridge a "manageable little drop." After performing a countdown from five, AJ threw himself over. "I felt the pull of the rubber cord attached to my back." Then the cord yanked him upward before he touched the Waitemata Harbor.

"It was fair to say I was sold on the idea right from the outset."

***

In the fall of 2005, I was on a week-long break from classes at the University of Canterbury as part of a five-month-long study abroad experience in Christchurch, New Zealand. In preparation for a pilgrimage to Queenstown—the so-called adventure capital of the world—I bought an old Subaru hatchback for $500 with a friend, splitting it down the middle. We loaded it up with friends and had another car follow us six hours south.

It wasn't hard to spot the AJ Hackett Bungee Center when we arrived in Queenstown. It was a kind of Mecca for adrenaline junkies, thrill-seekers, and hooligans—people like my friends and me. AJ says his target demographic was backpackers and leisure travelers. "People who are pretty much living a dream existence for a year or so."

I dropped a hefty sum of money on a package called the Thrillogy, which consisted of three bungee jumps spaced out over the course of the week. Our first jump was from the Kawaru Bridge, the world's first commercial bungee jumping site, established in 1988 by AJ Hackett and his partner Henry van Asch, co-founder of the business.

As a staff member tightened my harness, he asked, "Do you want to bob above the water, touch, or dunk?" I didn't think long. "Dunk me." He nodded. I stood up and hopped my way to the edge. The man holding the cord stood behind me and began the fast countdown: "Five-four-three-two-one." Without thinking, I jumped and plummeted 140 feet into the water, dunking myself in the lime-green Kawarau River below.

"There's a logical process to bungee jumping," AJ says. "Once you've done a couple jumps at any particular height, you want to go higher." After jumping from Auckland's Greenhithe Bridge, he and his friends upped the ante the next weekend and gathered on the ninety-eight-foot-high bridge in Hamilton, New Zealand. It was there AJ had his first run-in with the police. But when the cops arrived, they had no idea what to do, unsure if the thrill-seekers were breaking any laws. AJ told the cops he was reinventing adventure tourism and then offered them a jump. They turned him down but let AJ and his friends make the plunge anyway.

AJ chose Auckland's most visible structure next: the Harbour Bridge. It was a 131-foot jump, so he didn't want to "stuff it up." They choose a

Sunday. Why? Because there were fewer cops on Sunday. By that point, he understood the science of the cord so well that he was able to adjust it to dip in the water. AJ and his friends did a 262-foot jump next, which produced a powerful rebound and helped answer a few lingering unknowns with the bungee system.

The next time they jumped from the Auckland Harbour Bridge, the cops arrived by boat, demanding they stop. AJ leaped anyway. Chris recalled, "AJ went before me, straight into his headfirst dive, and I saw the coppers' jaws drop. All these police must have been thinking they were about to fish dead bodies out of the water." But like the incident before, the police weren't certain any laws had been broken. They asked the bungee team if they had been drinking. AJ said they'd had a glass of champagne.

"What's it like?" a cop asked.

"Bloody great," AJ replied.

**

It turns out AJ has a history of jumping-off stuff. "When we were kids, some of my mates and I would jump off things, often into water, and usually without serious injury." He was a typical Kiwi male, according to him. "Bit of an adventure buff, into rock climbing, speed skating, surfing, and anything else that involved initiative and exhilaration."

AJ worked construction for almost 4 years after high school, earning an apprenticeship as a carpenter following the mandatory 8,000 hours of work. On a whim, he answered a newspaper advertisement to work as an encyclopedia salesman. He turned out to be a talented salesman—almost too good, he admits, which made him uncomfortable. When he met his first great love, he quit the sales job and went in search of adventures, building a tiny house in the bed of a pickup truck. They toured New Zealand for about four years while AJ gradually built a construction business.

In his autobiography, AJ says his father was a quiet man, not particularly loving or communicative. It wasn't until a growth on his father's face began to rot that he visited a doctor. Though he underwent surgery for skin cancer, his condition was too advanced, and he later passed away.

"The lesson I learned from my relationship with my father was that you have two choices on this planet: You either love life to the max, or you simply exist." AJ's father simply existed, according to him. "He let his

The Dizziness of Freedom   21

loneliness beat him down. I swore when he died that I would live life to the max from that moment onwards."

***

My second bungee jump was at night, at the top of a hill just outside Queenstown's center. We took the Skyline Gondola to reach The Ledge, a small shack jutting about fifteen feet out into the air. According to AJ's website, the bungee jump was a true example of the Kiwi's "up-for-anything" attitude.

We stepped out of the gondola and were rewarded with panoramic views of the town below. The bungee harness was specially designed for the jump. It's strapped to your waist, giving you a good degree of creative freedom from the launch pad.

"Is it okay if I do a gainer?" I asked the staff member, referring to a maneuver where you jump forward and then rotate into a backflip.

"Yeah, mate," he said, tightening the harness around my waist. "But watch out for your head. I've seen people knock themselves out doing that trick."

I was the first to go of my friends. I huffed and puffed, then ran and leaped into the air and rotated backward. As I dropped into the blackness, there was a brief flash as the automatic camera captured the jump. I bought the picture after. It showed me inverted, the staff member's mouth open wide as he watched my head miss the platform by inches.

***

In 1987, AJ traveled to France as part of the New Zealand speed skiing team, a sport where competitors are ranked according to average speed over the course of 328 feet. "Racers start with a mammoth drop," AJ says, "tucking into the most aerodynamic position possible before the slope flattens. Then you hold your speed through a 330-foot timing trap."

On the side, AJ and his bungee jumping friends worked with experts to learn more about the rubber bungee material. For their first jump in France, AJ chose the massive Le Pont de la Caille Bridge, an abandoned 482-foot high suspension bridge. It was their highest jump yet—"a big bastard," in AJ's words. It was also the first time he performed the classic arms out, swallow dive. AJ's next jump was from a gondola, 298 feet in the air.

He dropped toward a blanket of powder, then smashed fists-first through snow. He had been learning karate, which helped, he said.

As the bungee jumping craze caught fire in France, more people began attending AJ's jumps. Many wanted to try it for themselves. During one jumping bonanza, a man was about to leap when AJ noticed that his cord wasn't attached. He was able to stop the man before he jumped, but the incident reinforced the importance of safety for AJ.

As the extreme sport gained popularity, a mass hysteria emerged, and AJ knew he could build a business around it. After he gave some of his French friends a few cords of their own, European bungee took off. "It was a radical acceleration from zero to 100 m.p.h.," AJ says. When it was time for the ski team to return home, AJ stayed, saying, "There was another tower in Paris I wanted to jump off."

***

Thousands of years ago, the sport of bungee jumping originated in the southern part of Pentecost Island in Vanuatu. Legend has it, a woman who was fleeing her abusive husband climbed to the top of a banyan tree to escape. The husband, Tamalie, found her there and climbed in pursuit. Reaching the top, Tamalie berated his wife, even dared her to jump. To his surprise, she did, cleverly tying two vines to her ankles. Tamalie didn't notice the vines and was amazed to see her reach ground unharmed. Not wanting to appear cowardly, he jumped as well, falling to his death.

The story gave rise to the annual land-diving event in Vanuatu. Over the course of ten days, during the village's Yam Harvest, the community constructs towers where young boys, newly circumcised, jump from the lower levels as an initiation to manhood. The ritual is believed to ensure a plentiful harvest, as well as improve the strength and health of the divers. It's also believed to ward off evil spirits, including Tamalie's spirit, which is believed to reside in the tower until all jumps have been performed.

The jump—which consists of leaping off a twenty- to thirty-foot-high tower and experiencing incredible g-forces as the vines pull taught at the bottom, missing the ground by inches—is considered an expression of one's boldness. Each jumper can decide to step down without shame or disgrace. They are not humiliated or considered cowards. Their choice is respected.

***

Søren Kierkegaard was a nineteenth-century Danish philosopher who explored the concept of choice. Every decision, he said, comes with absolute freedom of choice. According to Kierkegaard, when facing a decision we can either choose to do something, or nothing. Such freedom can cause anxiety, which he deemed the "dizziness of freedom."

In his book *The Concept of Anxiety*, Kierkegaard illustrates this point using an example of a man standing on a cliff who looks over the edge and experiences two fears. The first is the fear of falling. The second is the fear brought on by the impulse to throw himself off the edge. The man cannot deny that he could easily make the second choice, and that is anxiety-provoking, Kierkegaard claimed. It's the same choice before Shakespeare's Hamlet. Should Hamlet kill his uncle and avenge his father, or not? More profoundly, he asks, "To be, or not to be?"

The question, of course, is whether to choose life, or death.

According to Kierkegaard, being made aware of this freedom of choice increases our self-awareness and sense of personal responsibility. But no one can deny its dizzying effect, too, particularly at the edge of something high. Perhaps the appeal of bungee jumping is that it allows us to indulge this second, terrifying choice. We can throw ourselves off a high object free from the consequences.

In AJ's words: "Every ounce of your being tells you that deliberately tumbling off a high platform is the wrong thing to do. Having an opportunity to overcome that natural reaction is what makes bungee jumping such a special experience."

***

My last bungee jump in Queenstown, New Zealand, was the most epic: the highest in Australasia. To reach the Nevis bungee site, we took a van up the side of a mountain, passing through a series of perilous switchbacks with sheer cliffs on one side. Once or twice I thought our van was going to tumble off the ledge, never to be seen again.

When we reached the top, we saw a vast gorge with the Nevis River snaking through the forest 400 feet below. The staff split us into groups of six and loaded my group into a gondola-sized pod. The pod shuttled us across the gorge on a high wire and stopped in the middle. A section of the pod's floor was made of glass, which people circled around as if it were open air. I was called to a reclining chair, where a staff member strapped a huge cord to my ankles and tightened straps around my chest. I started to wonder if I was up for the challenge. Would I chicken out? I had that choice.

As I sat in the chair, deeply anxious, the staff yanked the cord across the pod's floor and lowered it off the pod toward the distant ground, 439 feet down. I unfolded myself out of the chair and hobbled to a small platform about shoulder width sticking out from the pod. I heard the countdown from some far-away place. Somehow, it helped. "Counting down gives you momentum and confidence," AJ says. "The countdown gives jumpers that little but of extra help in getting off the platform."

Against everything I knew to be right, I bent my knees and leaped off the ledge, bringing my arms into a swallow dive. I fell for eight seconds, then the cord recoiled, and I bounced a few times. As the staff pulled on my cord, I leaned toward my legs and unlatched my ankles so that I could invert myself and take in the awe-inspiring view.

***

To this day, AJ Hackett has broken every bungee jumping record you can break. In 1992, he won the Jack Newman Award for individual contribution to New Zealand tourism. Though he claims he could jump from anything with the right amount of planning, he admits, "I'm not that fussed about making any more big record-breaking jumps." Nowadays, he gets more satisfaction from "a nice little jump" he says, around 160–330 feet.

AJ and his business partner have seven AJ Hackett Bungy Sites around the world, including Australia, France, Germany, Indonesia, Macau, Malaysia, and the original site in Queenstown. Over two million people have jumped with the organization, and he continues to build his bungee empire. Every skyscraper or high-rise presents a high-adrenaline business opportunity.

"What other people see merely as a structure for beaming out radio waves or an observation platform with a revolving restaurant, I see as an untapped wonderland in a major city center." His adventure site in Macau, China, is a good example, where he built a 1,115-foot tower that provides a smattering of high-adrenaline activities, one of which includes the world's highest bungee jump, a mind-bending 764 feet.

***

On the day AJ bungee jumped off the Eiffel Tower, he awoke in the early morning and spotted his team at the base of the tower rolling up their sleeping bags and unpacking camera equipment. AJ's alarm hadn't gone off, so his ground team had been waiting an hour. Other people noticed the activity and began to gather, craning their heads upward curiously. AJ dressed in his tuxedo.

"From high up on the platform, I could see all this developing below," AJ says. There was no turning back now. Only one way down for me." He tested the height once more, lowering a nylon string from his perch. Then he heard voices, the chatter of staff climbing steps. Security shifts didn't start for a half hour, but he took evasive maneuvers, ducking behind metal girders. They passed, oblivious.

AJ did a few more safety checks, then bound his ankles with cord. He poured a glass of champagne and sipped silently. Then he set the glass down and hopped to the ledge. He stuck his toes over the ledge and leaped into the brisk morning air.

"The ground rushed up, and the four great struts disappeared out of the side of my vision." He fell for three seconds, the only person to have seen the Eiffel Tower from that perspective and lived to tell about it. "It's a hell of a beautiful site," he said.

The French police weren't as pleased as the daredevil. They ran toward the tower's center from all directions. As AJ sipped from a champagne bottle, the officers shouted and pointed, flabbergasted by what they had just witnessed. As they tried to figure out how to handle him, AJ did a quick interview for the cameras.

"What do you think the police will do, AJ?" the interviewer asked.

"They're reasonable people," AJ responded, "and I think they'll see this as an inspiration for the people of Paris and the world."

The police put AJ in a police van for questioning, but he wasn't there long. His friend, Sophie, showed the cops AJ's passport and a plane ticket back to New Zealand. AJ reiterated that he'd be out of the country in hours. Unsure of the legality of the situation, the cops let AJ go after about ten minutes.

The stunt put bungee jumping on the international stage, and New Zealanders were in love with AJ and the extreme sport he pioneered.

Footage of the stunt was broadcasted across the world and captured on the front page of the France Soir, the headline reading, "Un Kiwi a fait le yo-yo du haut de la Tour Eiffel."

"We were blessed that day," AJ said. "Fortune favors the brave."

CHAPTER 4

A Taste of Glory

When I woke up on the day of the Newport marathon in Rhode Island, I hadn't planned to run 26.2 miles in under four hours. In the five months of training, the thought hadn't crossed my mind once. When I decided to go for it, it was an hour before the start of the race, and I was staring at a plate of scrambled eggs. If I could finish a marathon in less than four hours, I thought it might trigger a tremendous feeling of accomplishment.

The physical benefits of running are all well and good, but I don't run to get in shape. It's not my escape or meditation. It's the spiritual rewards I'm after. I run to pursue what the psychologist Abraham Maslow called a "peak experience." Time slows down during a peak experience. For that reason, it's often associated with flow state, the feeling of being totally absorbed in an activity.

Maslow sometimes referred to a peak experience as the "oceanic feeling" in which your consciousness expands, you feel interconnected, at peace. But these experiences are elusive. According to the psychologist, only 2 percent of the population has ever had one.

The marathon began at 8 a.m. in downtown Newport, Rhode Island. When the gun fired, five thousand runners left Easton's Beach jogging into a salty breeze, down tight roads hugging the ocean and past sand dunes and bushes, cottages, and rolling hills. It seemed fertile ground for an oceanic feeling.

Before Maslow began his study of peak experiences, he assumed they only happened to saints and mystics. But he found that peak experiences weren't religious in nature. In interviews, people from all walks of life reported blissful moments—times when they felt limitless and enormously powerful. "Anything that feels close to perfect triggers a peak experience," said Maslow. Triggers include sex, nature, and music. Maslow spoke with a teenage football player who had a peak experience after scoring a touchdown on a breakaway run.

Consciously or unconsciously, I think we all have a deep desire for these psychological elixirs. They can replace our drab, mundane existence with a brilliant flash of glory. The mythologist Joseph Campbell touched on this universal desire when he wrote:

> *People say that what we're all seeking is a meaning for life. I don't think that's what we're really seeking. I think that what we're seeking is an experience of being alive, so that our life experiences on the purely physical plane will have resonances with our own innermost being and reality, so that we actually feel the rapture of being alive.*

At their worst, peak experiences lodge themselves in our consciousness forever and live on as a wonderful memory. At their best, they go to work on you, and can have a transforming effect. The psychiatrist William Miller said a peak experience can stimulate "quantum change." Such is their therapeutic value. In a world where changes are usually small and incremental, a peak experience has the awesome power to trigger a radical shift in consciousness, instantly. While there's no formula for manufacturing a peak experience, most of us have a general sense of our own triggers.

Running, I've found, is my drug of choice.

The Newport Marathon is referred to as a "destination race" for good reason. Keeping a fast pace, I passed some of the most scenic locations in the iconic New England town. We jogged through Newport's city center, down the historic Thames Street, hugged by shops, restaurants, inns, and colonial buildings, some of which date back to the seventeenth and eighteenth centuries. We circled around Fort Adams State Park, passing picnickers enjoying panoramic views of Newport Harbor.

We passed the Newport Country Club and the famous clubhouse, a mansion built in the classic Beaux Arts style. We ran along Ocean Drive, which gave us spectacular views of beaches and the Atlantic Ocean. We then turned onto Bellevue Avenue and marveled over the opulent mansions. At mile thirteen, the course folded back toward the starting line, and I felt stronger than I'd expected to feel. However, at mile nineteen, my body staged a revolt in the form of cramping legs, hobbling me every few minutes until the tightness in my hamstrings released.

Just as I had started to make peace with the fact that I wouldn't finish the race in less than four hours, I asked a nearby runner if he was trying to keep a pace.

"Four hours," he said, coincidently. "If you stay with me, you'll do it, too."

I told him I'd try to keep up, thinking perhaps a peak experience was still within reach.

With three miles left, I had lost sight of the runner, but I knew I was close to my goal. As I turned the last corner, I saw the time of 3:55, and I got my trigger.

Suddenly, I felt spread out and light. The backs of my eyes became wet. I felt electric. As I crossed the finish line in a state of bliss, I knew I was having a peak experience. I was changing, quantum-style.

CHAPTER 5

A Lesson in Safety

When I bought a motorcycle in my early thirties, everyone thought I was going to die. I became a cautionary tale for friends, family, and colleagues: a dead man riding. I was no longer a rational, sane person in their eyes; I had become a cowboy, a reckless simpleton—destined to hurt myself or worse.

Wanting to rebel against the overly safe people in my life, I set off on my maiden voyage only hours after my brother taught me how to ride. Leaving Cambridge, I steered my 1982 Honda Nighthawk onto Massachusetts Route 2 and began the half-hour drive to Concord, stomping grounds of Henry David Thoreau, who wrote *Civil Disobedience*. This, I had decided, would be my own refusal to obey conventional wisdom.

It's just this kind of hubris that often gets people into trouble. The Ancient Greeks warned about such overconfidence. Shakespeare wrote dramas about pride preceding epic failures. Hollywood has grown rich by creating characters who fly too close to the sun. I knew this when I set out. I knew the risks and the dangers, but I was committed to making the journey anyway.

About a mile into the trip, I pulled into a gas station and quickly realized I didn't know how to put gas in the machine. Once I'd figured it out, I knew I hadn't parked close enough to the pump. Instead of repositioning the bike, I pulled the hose tight and leaned into the motorcycle, touching my calf to the searing muffler. A patch of my skin liquefied. The injury was a bad omen, and I should have turned back then. I didn't.

Was everyone's caution justified? Now, I had never actually ridden a motorcycle before buying one. The purchase resulted from weeks of musing on Robert M. Pirsig's *Zen and the Art of Motorcycle Maintenance*. In one of the book's philosophical discussions, Pirsig categorized people into two types of thinkers: classical and romantic. He used a motorcycle as a metaphor to illustrate the differences between the two.

To the classical thinker, a motorcycle is a collection of moving parts that work together as an understandable mechanism. Should the bike break down, a classical thinker is keen to diagnose the mechanical issue and attempt to repair it themselves.

For the romantic thinker, a motorcycle is more than the sum of its parts. A romantic cares less about how a bike works than what it represents, where it can take them, and how it can make them feel when they're riding. Should it break down, a romantic seeks a mechanic to take care of repairs. They have no interest in diagnosing problems, and they won't tinker.

After reading Pirsig's book, I knew I was a romantic. I didn't care how my motorcycle worked; I just wanted to see where it could take me.

When I first told people I'd gotten the bike, I thought I could explain away their negative reactions with Pirsig's personality model. I figured I was just surrounded by classical thinkers. However, I wanted to understand where everyone's skepticism came from, so I began running an experiment.

With some people, I would act cavalier. "I just bought a motorcycle," I might announce with a proud grin. As expected, this invited cautionary tales. Everyone knew someone who had had an accident on two wheels.

"See you at your funeral," was my best friend's response.

With others, I would act meek and uneasy. Their reactions were subtler, but they all still thought I was an idiot. "Please be careful," most pleaded. "Make sure you wear a helmet," was a common remark. Those who worked in health care really gave it to me. Before I could say, "Don't worry; I'll wear a helmet," they would fire off their most horrific emergency room stories.

It didn't matter if I was proud or thoughtful; a motorcycle was bad news.

Having obtained my learner's permit and passed the licensing test, I knew the dangers of operating a motorcycle. I knew that one in ten accidents involved a bike and that motorcyclists were thirty-five times more likely to experience a deadly accident than car drivers. By reading the Massachusetts motorcycle manual, I also learned that head injuries were the leading cause of death in motorcycle crashes. Wearing a helmet reduced the chances of death by 37 percent.

Intersections could be especially perilous because motorcycles were smaller and harder to see coming. And the common saying "speed kills" was based on the truth: Half of all motorcycle accidents didn't even involve other vehicles. Finally, it was extremely ill-advised—and, of course, illegal—to drink alcohol and get on a motorcycle. In 2020 alone, 5,268 motorcycle operators were killed in traffic crashes, of which 27 percent—1,436—had a blood alcohol level above the legal limit of 0.8.

During conversations, I explained that I'd wear a helmet, I would always look both ways going through intersections, and I would never drink and drive. So why was everyone still so afraid for me?

Maybe it wasn't the motorcycle but rather me. I had just turned 30; did they all see this as my last-ditch effort to delay becoming an adult? Was I just being a contrarian—again? Or maybe it was because I didn't always wear a seatbelt at that time in my life, and they knew it.

I also wondered if it was just a case of country boy versus city folk. Having grown up in northern New Hampshire, I strongly identify with the state's motto, "Live free or die." Many people who had grown up in or around Massachusetts thought the saying was too black-and-white, cavalier, and foolish even. I had trouble explaining to them that all I really wanted from a motorcycle was a new experience of road travel, an organic taste of the outdoors, and a bit of novelty.

Despite my bravado, I got the distinct feeling I was in over my head when I hit Route 2. I was struck by how exposed I was on a motorcycle. There really was nothing between me and the possibility of a lot of pain. It wasn't until I arrived in Concord's city center that I realized how tightly I was gripping the handlebars.

Before I left Cambridge, I had considered myself a poster child for living on the edge. A modern-day transcendentalist! By the time I reached my destination, I was deeply shaken. The ride had scared me. I walked the streets of Concord aimlessly, delaying my return trip.

The decision to take the journey, I realized, had been rather *unsafe* of me.

On the eventual ride home, I gained some confidence and allowed myself to reflect on the idea of safety and how being cautious had its merits. It kept us alive, for one thing. But one could also be *too* safe and take no journeys at all.

When I arrived home an hour later, I thought about Thoreau and how he had gone to the woods to "drive life into a corner and reduce it to its lowest terms." Sometimes, life can drive you into a corner and reduce you to your lowest terms. Life can scare you. Motorcycles can scare you. But I think it's better to scare yourself now and again than to be afraid of being scared.

"Living is so dear" that Thoreau did not "wish to practice resignation." Like Thoreau, "I did not wish to live what was not life" nor "discover that I had not lived" upon my death. A little bit of danger, I had found, was worth the risk.

CHAPTER 6

Missing Paris

The day before I ran the Paris Marathon, I visited the race's expo in a gigantic convention center. Strolling from vendor to vendor, I stopped at a massive poster the race organizers had created for the almost 40,000 runners. Alphabetized and written horizontally across the poster were the names of every runner.

Superimposed over the names was the marathon route through Paris, a thick white line that happened to obscure an unlucky few. I watched as participants pointed gleefully at their names, making peace signs or a thumbs up for cameras. Some growled as the great white route bulldozed through a letter in their name. My name was nowhere to be found. It was completely covered by the route.

For the Marathon de Paris, runners must show their race bibs to a volunteer before they can squeeze through a narrow opening in a ten-foot-high fence to join the other participants. After you cross the threshold, you become a kind of wild park animal for friends, family, and spectators dangling from windows and sipping espressos in cafés. The pictures that day have the absurd familiarity of a zoo. Me, hopping in place, making goofy faces and tongues at the camera.

It was Sunday, a little after 8:00 a.m. I emerged from the Metro, stepped onto the Avenue des Champs Élysées, and gazed up at the Arc de Triomphe, where the 26.2-mile race began and ended. There was a palpable buzz in the air for the fifth-largest marathon in the world, a whirling electricity of nerves and exhilaration.

I sympathized with any shop owner with a toilet. Runners bunched up in droves outside bathroom doors, staring at the floor, tapping their feet as Nature called. "Sir?" a waiter asked me, raising his finger as I darted through the front door of a café. But I was already halfway down the steps, a bit ashamed. I joined the long line for the bathroom and rejoiced every time a flush rang out. It turns out the bladder wasn't equipped to store two coffees, a full sports drink, and who knows how many anxious gulps of bottled water.

As I slipped through the gate, I joined thousands of runners bunched into different start zones grouped by self-predicted finish times. I had chosen the four-hour, thirty-minute zone based on my two previous marathons, where I had run 4:10 in Hyannis, Massachusetts, and 3:55 in Newport, Rhode Island. It was a respectable category, I thought, one that conformed to my original plan of just taking the whole thing easy. It was April, and the morning air was frigid. I watched people bounce in place and blow into cupped fingers. Some folded their legs in half, stretching. Others crossed their arms and studied the pavement. Doubled up on fleeces, I rubbed my hands together vigorously.

Looking around, I felt like I had attended a Halloween party without a costume. A young man next to me wore a pink bunny suit. The man in front of him had donned a Superman costume. There was a group of girls dressed as cocktail waitresses and a group of guys in banana suits. I saw a woman in a business suit and a man in wig, even someone wearing the Eiffel Tower.

To energize us, a spirited race volunteer stood atop a metal crate and shouted encouraging words through a loudspeaker, none of which I could understand because it was in French. Clapping and dancing to blaring techno music, the announcer managed to synchronize most of us into a jumping jacks routine and then a kind of flash dance.

Minutes later, I heard the gunfire, but I didn't move. I couldn't. There were literally thousands of people bunched up in front of me. I had to wait almost thirty minutes before the waves cleared out. As I crossed the starting line with fellow runners shouting and holding their hands high, I witnessed the marvelous city in glorious fashion.

Ten minutes into the race, I found a rhythm, happy to be warm. I took a sip of water and scampered down a hill, rubbing shoulders with other runners. I circled the obelisk in the Place de Concorde and turned onto Rue de Rivoli. The Champs-Elysées opened into five or six lanes, and people began to create cushions of space. The course was flat, never higher than 200 feet, and straightforward. Seven miles in, I passed through the Bois de Vincennes. I was strangely okay with the fact that I still had to jog more miles than most people's daily commutes.

The route took us by countless fountains, manicured trees, cinemas, gardens, museums, galleries, and cafés. Half the fun was admiring the creativity of the spectators hugging the road. According to the race website, there were between 200,000 and 240,000 spectators present for the citywide party.

While running, I locked eyes with an elderly woman in a red and white costume. She was stomping her feet and somehow fashioning a melody with two wooden dowels. I smiled and ate an energy gel, losing myself in the musical acts and stunning architecture, the shouting crowds, and the huffing and puffing of racers.

Like river logs nearing a smaller stream, the course narrowed and funneled us into a tunnel—one of many in the race. The sun ducked away as I entered the tunnel and came shoulder to shoulder with strangers, close enough I could almost smell the mashed bananas on the soles of their shoes.

Separating us briefly from the spectators, the tunnel provided a profound camaraderie, a visceral we-are-in-this-together bond between those crazy enough to run almost thirty miles in a single day. I turned off the music in my headphones and heard heavy breathing echo off the brick walls and mix with the slapping of hundreds of pairs of sneakers against the cobblestone street. In the middle of the tunnel, someone let out a war cry. Another joined in, and then everyone was shouting triumphantly.

As I exited the tunnel, a man passed me, his eyes fixed on his watch. Others were similarly glued to their ticking clocks, calculating their paces obsessively, watching their heart rates like an emergency room doctor monitors a patient during intubation. As the man patted his belt, holding neatly stored energy packets, I wondered what phrase he might be whispering to himself. "Don't go out too fast," perhaps.

I was just glad to be there. And then it happened. Something awful. I saw *her*.

She wasn't hard to pick out of the crowd. People huddled around her like mothers clutching infants in hopes of getting a kiss from the Pope. She was the pacesetter—a trim, athletic woman with a pole attached to her back. At the top of the pole was a flag maybe six feet above her that said, "4:00 hr."

In that moment, I made the decision to pass her and stay past her.

Three years ago, I had somehow managed to run the Newport, Rhode Island, in under four hours. I'm a rugged fellow, built for power not endurance, so I've always been into contact sports—football in high school, rugby in college. Beating the mythical four-hour mark in Newport was a sheer display of willpower—and luck. I remember planning to enjoy that race, too. That was until I asked a fit older man the time. He told me he was on pace to break four hours. I followed him, and I ran a 3:55. I remember tearing up as I neared the finish line, in awe that my legs hadn't become traitorous and folded as I desperately tried to hit some target time for which my body had no interest.

My plan with the Paris marathon was to enjoy it, but I have a pattern for flip-flopping on race day. As I accelerated past the pacesetter, I decided to beat the four-hour mark again—maybe even set a personal best. I adopted a Spartan-like concentration and mumbled some platitude to myself like, "Pain is weakness leaving the body." I gained five, maybe ten minutes on the pacesetter and felt my confidence grow. But as I fantasized about the goal, Paris's beauty slipped away. Everything slid to the periphery, subservient to the new objective I'd set for myself.

In a place you could spend a lifetime admiring, I was too absorbed to notice any of its gifts, off in a dream. Basically, I was absent. I also started to undervalue accomplishments like passing the half marathon mark. As I reached this milestone in the heart of Paris, I said, "Thirteen more to go," and dug in.

I heard spectators shout my name because it was written on the race bib, but their voices were far away. I gave a child a high five, but the boy might as well have been a mannequin. I even ignored the Eiffel Tower as it came into view. No longer was the engineering masterpiece an iconic symbol to admire, but rather a momentary pause from ruminations of steamrolling across the finish line better, faster, stronger.

Every 3.1 miles were refueling stations. Like the tunnels, they created their own bottlenecks. As I neared a station around the fifteen-mile mark, I was overcome with conflicting desires. On the one hand, there was the primal urge to satisfy depleted sugar demands, but there was also the compulsion to waste no time. These competing demands, when multiplied across countless other racers, many of whom are hooked to their own time goals, created an unbelievable carnage, like a fisherman knocking a bucket of chum into a patch of ocean infested with sharks.

At the station, I absorbed an elbow from an eager runner cutting and shoving his way to the table. He grabbed a handful of raisins and shoved them into his mouth. To avoid much of the mayhem, all one would have to do is stop at the table further down the line where it's less populated with wild runners. But we didn't. We were on schedule. On pace. I ducked behind the raisin bandit and snagged a banana and an orange slice. I bit into the orange slice and slid out of the chaos. As I left the station, I watched runners toss plastic cups aside, rarely hitting one of the several trashcans.

It was around mile seventeen or eighteen when the pacesetter caught up to me. I tried to speed up, but my legs seized like an engine stuck in second gear. My legs were shot, presumably from pushing too hard, too fast. Eventually, the pacesetter got away from me, and I watched the four-hour flag bob out of sight. It was then that I made my second game-time decision. I let go of the goal. I detached myself from the pacesetter and the racers around me, and suddenly, the city of Paris came back into focus.

With over ninety musical groups on the streets, I heard melodies from full orchestras to lone drummer boys, from hooligans blowing horns to street musicians strumming violas. The crowd was filled with characters. A group of women in blue wigs shaking white pompoms. Soldiers in black uniforms and high white socks. A man dressed as a butler sipping champagne from a glass. Streaming from a wire across the road were 112 flags representing all the participating countries. The dance groups and rock bands helped with the misery of endurance running, shifting my attention from cramping legs.

I came to a refueling station, but this time was different than the others. I avoided the madness at the front of the line and dipped in at the end. I saw a man cramping, so I gave him a sodium tablet and wished him luck. I probably wouldn't have done that with a time goal.

The end of the Paris marathon felt a bit anticlimactic, much different than the Newport marathon, where I'd had what felt like a peak experience.

The last few hundred feet of the Paris marathon came down the Avenue Foch. Several miles from the finish line, I had hoped and begged for the end, but when it came, it just came.

As I crossed the finish line, I took a mighty breath and nodded to myself proudly. I watched other runners finish their marathons with their own triumphant gestures: a fist to the sky, a single finger overhead. Though there were infinite variations for demonstrating personal glory, there seemed to be one shared sentiment: relief.

Our bodies and minds were no longer being called on anymore, no longer subjected to extreme fixation. Perhaps this is why that glass of beer after the race felt like the best beer I'd ever had. Too exhausted to focus on anything else, my mind couldn't fixate on anything but that beer. Pleasantly captive to the present moment, I *really* tasted it.

Months after the race, I was home reading about the Paris Marathon. I learned that some of the refueling stations throughout the marathon had actually served cider, beer, wine, and even oysters. I also read that the race organizers had even set up a tent at the finish line for foot massages facing the Eiffel Tower.

My mind must have been somewhere else. I hadn't even noticed.

CHAPTER 7

The Hate Game

"Let's play a game," she said, bringing a cigarette to her lips. I took a sip from my beer and asked her what game she meant. She leaned forward in the green sofa chair. "First, I'll tell you what I hate about you," she said. "Then you tell me what you hate about me."

It was our first weekend as roommates, the ink still fresh on a one-year lease agreement. We sat on the porch that had already become our sanctuary—part clubhouse, part therapist's office. We dressed it up with a shaggy red carpet, sprinkled Christmas lights around the perimeter, and tucked the sofa chair in the corner. That night we started a dialogue, a series of conversations that began with tearing each other down, so that later we could build each other back up.

Our paths had crossed in the marketing department of a global research company. She—I'll call her Jade—operated a phone in the call center, and I wrote marketing copy. Jade was attractive with long dark hair, which she joked was "G-rated" because it was long enough to cover her breasts. Her stormy disposition was often matched by her dark wardrobe, and I noticed that in meetings, she didn't snicker at unfunny jokes—while everyone else faked it, she seemed unable to laugh unless she was sincerely amused.

I think she found my sunny temperament and vanilla exterior annoying at first. I was some Golden Boy, who, generally speaking, got what he put his mind to. But when we chatted in the halls at work, there was a resonance, the alchemy of kindred spirits. A defensive banter drew us together, the somewhat sarcastic humor that meant we played by similar rules. In that banter, though, there was also a lingering sadness, as if we had both been "cool kids" once, but somewhere along the way had lost our mojo.

That summer, I popped the question. Since our leases were both ending, would she be my roommate? We scanned apartment listings on Craigslist and then spent the weekend crisscrossing Boston in her Audi, meeting real estate brokers. "We're going to write our memoirs about this," I remember saying in jest, perhaps subconsciously recognizing that she had already become my muse. We found an apartment with a porch, which seemed like a fine place for cold drinks and deep conversations. It would be a place for retreat, reflection. It was home.

The next day, I broke the news to my work friends over lunch, and I got some news in return. Apparently, my new roommate's father ran one of the departments at the company; her uncle was the CEO, and her grandfather founded the now-billion-dollar enterprise. My boss seemed particularly skeptical of the proposed arrangement, saying, "I'll get the popcorn ready."

As the summer progressed and our September move-in date approached, the friendship blossomed. I met her mother at a party held by her grandmother, who lived in an affluent neighborhood in Boston. I could tell her mom thought our decision was hasty. Our connection whiffed of puppy love. She asked her daughter, "Are you sure you're still going to feel the same way in a few months?"

Jade's father was an easier sell. In her online dating profiles, Jade never fails to note that her dad is the funniest man she knows. The embodiment of cool, he can always make her laugh, often in the most peculiar of ways. One running joke implies his daughter's promiscuity. "You know how you get," he likes to say with a smirk, even if she was telling the most prudish of stories about a recent date. To him, if you aren't cool, you are a dweeb. And he wouldn't have his daughter shacking up with some dweeb. When I first crossed paths with him in the company's cafeteria, we shook hands and exchanged pleasantries. I didn't appear to be a dweeb, so I had his blessing.

Weeks into living together, Jade and I had hundreds of inside jokes. We bonded over horror films and fast-food runs. We made obscene jokes. We both liked the rock band Queen. We had lengthy discussions about why candy corn was only sold in the fall. She began referring to me as "Dustball."

Everyone waited for the announcement that we had coupled up. Or, at the very least, that we'd given each other "sensations," a term Jade used for "hooking up." But sensations were not exchanged, and an announcement never came. We openly discussed how "something" might happen and even played married when we went to bars. Sometimes we hugged, but on her terms only.

More so than her father, the man on Jade's pedestal was her grandfather, a noble, highly successful founder of the company for which we both worked. He had spent his long life deeply in love with a wife who freshened her lipstick every day before he walked through the door after work. He gave her everything, using his wealth to protect her from the inconveniences of daily living by making sure everything was taken care of. They were happily married for sixty years. Jade's soulmate needed her grandfather's buttoned-up ambitions and her father's rebellious spirit. Good Boy meets Bad Boy ... with an MBA.

There were stark differences between Jade's and my upbringing. My New England origins are decidedly blue-collar, rooted in a middle-to-lower-class existence in New Hampshire's White Mountains. She came from a middle-to-upper-class household in the suburbs of an affluent town in Massachusetts. Her dad showed great affection for sports cars and luxury watches. My dad adored mountain bikes and motorcycles. Jade's a fashionista; dressing rooms make me sweat. To me, life is an adventure. To her, life is absurd. I talk about things I love. She talks about things she hates.

Our differences did cause friction. Sometimes a stuck-up princess squabbled with a simple-minded brute—over splitting the cost of the television, painting the living room, and buying furniture. I insisted we find used items on Craigslist, she needed brand new. During a disagreement, a toxic cloud would descend upon the house, and we'd go a day or two without talking. Doors would bang with extra force. Shared TV time would cease. We'd scoot through communal areas and observe radio silence at work. And then someone would mutter something sarcastic, and the good times would return.

We found common ground in weirdness. Our gift was improvisation, and we used our talents to go to absurd places. If a screen door shut on its own, it was the clever work of a demon. Before we left the apartment, even though it was only us, we would ask if "everyone" was ready to leave.

"Ready to go, guys?" she'd ask.

I'd grin at her and look around the room. "Guys?"

We assembled strings of ridiculous ideas that I'm sure no one else ever thought of, which brought on deep belly laughs—part surprise, part admiration. We were masters of deadpan, and we used our best stuff on each other often. It was the driest kind of humor, and it was given free rein in our home.

Sometimes silly insights revealed profound truths. Jade's idea about "bursting someone's bubble" led her to announce that "bubbles" are precious. "All we have in life are our bubbles." That launched a discussion on the nature of hope. Often, silliness led to analysis. Whether it was a text, a reality TV show, or a social norm, we'd examined them in depth and excavate the underlying truths, often finding absurdity.

Much of this happened on the porch. I drank IPAs and she knocked down Red Bulls, sometimes three at a sitting. She burned through cigarettes and supplemented with popsicles. In one sitting, she might eat ten or more of them. I learned about her problems with alcohol, the days in rehab, and the "broken people" she had met. I learned about medications she'd taken, like Adderall and Klonopin.

It seemed that she had made an art of rumination and typically believed everything she thought. It was a habit that fueled bouts of depression. She told me about her years in therapy. At that time, I had little understanding—and tolerance—for therapy. It seemed pointless, even self-indulgent. Let the past be the past, I'd say. She detested this perspective, dismissing it as naive and perhaps a rejection of her experience and life.

Eventually, Jade relaxed her own no-drinking policy and would have a glass of wine for our sessions on the porch. It wasn't falling off the wagon, I liked to think. Rather, our friendship and home had provided a warm, safe place to develop new habits with old substances.

On the porch, Jade and I discussed the concept of "dark sides." I wasn't so sure we all had them at the time. I was fresh out of graduate school and heavy into the personal development literature. I was a few years past my New Age and "spiritual texts" phases and had just left a year-long phase exploring Ancient Greek philosophy. Puffed up on timeless wisdom, I might respond to Jade's confessions with axioms such as "change your thinking," because, as many great luminaries have professed: "We are what we repeatedly think."

She rejected these quips as intellectual crutches. Perhaps, she suggested, these clichés were defenses against going too deep within myself? A way of avoiding real feelings? Her objections made me think. For all of our differences, I came to see us as two sides of the same coin. She was depressed, admittedly; I was grandiose, blindly. When we played The Hate Game, it forced me to acknowledge flaws and weaknesses I couldn't admit I had. It urged me to confront a self that often took itself too seriously, that could be at times patronizing, that had an elevated sense of self-worth, and perhaps required admiration as emotional fuel. Whenever I rooted myself in a platitude, Jade would begin the game and sling arrows at a dark red bullseye on my chest, making me question the self I'd stitched together with self-help books and ancient knowledge.

The catharsis The Hate Game triggered often gave way to antidotes. Whenever I lifted off into illusions, Jade injected realism and reminded me of the ground beneath my feet. Whenever daily struggles overwhelmed her, I suggested taking action on the things she could control, and if no action was possible at that time, to try and put the problem out of her mind. We kept each other in check and the melancholy we first recognized in each other's eyes began to melt. We were getting our mojo back.

And then I fell in love. With someone else. I'll call her Paige.

Paige was a graduate student at Tufts studying Occupational Therapy. She was my type: brunette, petite, and athletic, and I admired her academic excellence, ambition, and intelligence. Funny and intense, I also liked how she could bounce from sarcasm to sweetness without a glitch. To me, she was beautiful. Beauty involves more than being externally attractive—beauty is an air, in my opinion. Perhaps I'm referring to some traditional notion of femininity—gentle, sensitive, empathetic—but what I find most beautiful is equanimity, or a calmness of mind.

"Do you think I'm beautiful?" Jade once asked me. While I'd always thought she was something of a vixen, I had never used the word "beautiful," I think because she was missing the poise or grace I found so attractive in Paige. Jade's mind was ever on fire, her body always following her brain, like a pinball in the drama of her own thoughts. As corny as it sounds, Jade was most "beautiful" to me when she was rubbing her dog's face. How could her mind possibly be anywhere else in a moment like that?

"What I am going to say may seem ... offensive," I said in response to Jade's question on beauty, but it was in the spirit of The Hate Game. I told her she reminded me of Naomi Watts's character at the beginning of the film, *The Painted Veil*. Watts plays an immature, spoiled Englishwoman named Kitty Fane. By likening Jade to Kitty, I was telling her I thought she still had some growing up to do. Jade hadn't seen the movie, thank God. "Watch it, though, something to think about."

Meanwhile, Paige and I went headlong into a love affair. The kind of romance where you stare at each other as you walk away in parting and then jog back for one last kiss. *I like you ... I love you ... let's get married ... let's make a baby*. A year into our relationship, Paige had our names etched onto a padlock, which we attached to the Pont des Arts Bridge, or "The Love Bridge," in Paris while on vacation. We took a picture of us holding the keys over the railing and then tossed them into the Seine River.

When Paige first met Jade, she said it seemed like the two of us were a couple. Paige saw the obvious chemistry. The banter, the inside jokes. She watched me work around Jade's moods. And Jade and I were living together, after all.

Jade had her opinion of Paige, too. While she adored Paige, I remember Jade delicately trying to address the idea that Paige might be, well, sort of dull, perhaps not dynamic enough for someone with a creative personality like mine. There was a plainness to Paige's personality, I supposed, but I thought she was wholesome, and I was romanced by her formal values, traditional upbringing, and exceedingly kind family. I also wondered that after several months of living with Jade, perhaps I wanted a woman less dramatic, more "normal," even a bit dull, to use Jade's word.

Whenever the three of us hung out together, Paige would sometimes tiptoe around Jade, who could be hard to predict. Like when Jade might shout "bored" if a conversation wasn't stimulating enough for her. Over time, I began to see similarities between the two women. Though cheerful most of the time, Paige's moods occasionally sunk to surprising lows: sudden crying in the passenger seat of my car, wanting to sleep longer than usual on a Sunday morning, or silences for no discernable reason. Paige had a lot of Jade's darkness without the oddities.

When the lease on our apartment ended, Jade and I decided to find separate homes. She bought a condo in Boston's South End. I found a place to share with roommates in Cambridge, not far from Paige. As luck would have it, Jade and I were both promoted into the executive building at the company, where we sat in cubicles fifteen feet apart, allowing the fun to continue.

Months later for Jade's birthday, we saw a Queen tribute band. Over familiar tunes, we mourned the loss of the porch and shared stories of the good ole days. She was thriving, with a puppy and a chic condo. Nearly finished with a master's degree in communications, she had also joined a gym and was having a steamy fling with a twenty-something who was "so cute, but sort of boring," and importantly, not a dweeb. That night, I gave her a birthday card that sang Queen's "You're my best friend" when opened.

Much to Jade's disappointment, Paige and I made plans to move out of Massachusetts. We went state shopping—Colorado, California, Washington—and let the job applications fly. Paige got a job offer in Portland, Oregon, and I got an offer down the block from where I lived. We poured champagne. We became bicoastal. We'd make it.

Driven by several months of loneliness, I decided to do something I'd never done before: seek out psychotherapy. The therapist I found was a kind and intelligent social worker who listened to me with rapt attention, never judging. In therapy, I found myself talking less about the obvious difficulties Paige and I were facing and more about the detritus Jade and I had churned up during The Hate Game. With my therapist as a guide, I became a cartographer, mapping the shadowed places of my life.

As I racked up sessions, I realized that life's struggles had their ways of leaving cuts in our psyches. Whether these psychic cuts are narrow or gaping, if they aren't cleaned, dressed, and bandaged with some level of care, they can fester and threaten the integrity of the whole. Jade was the first who urged me to look at the cuts I'd endured when I was young; my therapist kept the ball rolling.

We explored my parent's divorce when I was around 6 years old. We talked about my mother's substance abuse and depression and her absence for a year or so. I began to question the virtue of The Stick, a slim piece of wood my father retrieved when, for example, I accidentally tossed a shoe through a bay window, aiming for my brother.

Months into therapy, I broke down over the loss of my grandmother, Anne, who'd helped raise me in the turmoil of divorce. Anne provided care and love for me when my parents could not. She would always slice the crust from my grilled cheese sandwiches, and each Halloween transformed her porch into an elaborate haunted house. I can still hear her Siamese cat's low, achy meow in my mind. I was 17 years old when Anne died of lung cancer. I hadn't dealt with it until now.

Making a map of an amnesic childhood takes a village, and I soon realized that my parents had all the keys to the locked doors in my mind. Whenever I'd visit, I would ambush them on fact-finding missions, sometimes with the harmless air of curiosity, other times with the fierceness of a prosecutor. The introspective exercise was as foreign to them as The Hate Game had been to me, but they tried to entertain my questions as best they could. Knowing the painful history and my inquisitive nature, I think they both half-expected me to circle back with questions at some point.

Six months into therapy, I began to realize that a healthy family environment might look a lot like Paige's—safe, predictable, nurturing. In childhood, each of my parents would move every few years. Just when I had memorized the contours of a backyard, I had to pack up my ball and play somewhere else. If my brother or I acted out—perhaps by destroying the inner workings of our father's well by dropping rocks down it—there was The Stick. In our household, love wasn't discussed and rarely felt.

To help describe how I was feeling, I started to build a new psychological vocabulary. I learned terms like repression, shame, guilt, denial. I learned new ideas and theories such as Attachment Disorder and "narcissistic tendencies" and made a hobby out of researching adverse childhood experiences and how they can influence one's behavior in adulthood. A week after taking a six-hour long psychological assessment, a psychiatrist delivered her conclusion: repressed anger and sadness. "That's really heavy," I said, my eyes unexpectedly welling up.

I brought my report into therapy, and slowly, over time, I processed its findings and began applying Band-Aids to old wounds.

A year into therapy, I was starting to see things more clearly. I could be more honest with myself. I knew my long-distance relationship with Paige had become dysfunctional. We were calling each other less and planning fewer visits. As the foundation of our relationship started crumbling, we became distant. Eventually, Paige and I both strayed. And then it was over.

In therapy, I realized that I had been lonely when I met Paige and had become even more so since she moved away. I had fallen for her wholesome upbringing because it was the opposite of mine. I also think there was some truth to the notion that perhaps she had been acting out the depressive aspects of my grandiosity, a side of my personality that I had been steadily trying to erode.

When I told Jade about the breakup, she wasn't in the best of places either. Mr. Cute and Boring hadn't worked out, and she was accumulating unfulfilling relationships. When she and I arrived at a liquor store one night, she insisted I enter by myself, because she was afraid the cashiers would judge her at seeing another new companion. You know how you get, I joked. But it was no laughing matter. Jade was spiraling.

Intending to cheer each other up, we planned a Saturday of delights. After an afternoon of Prosecco and red wine, we welcomed the night with beers and vodka tonics. I told her about the progress I was making in therapy. She told me about her recent struggles with drinking, with men, with sadness. Even though she had spent most of her adult life in therapy, I realized she still had unexplored areas of her psyche, one of them being the man who occasionally reminded her of "how she gets." She used to push me to address my illusions, so I pushed her to examine hers.

The conversation started with Jade's most recent breakup. The relationship had been going well until she began poking holes in it. Eventually, like the others, it blew up. It seemed kind of self-sabotaging, I said, suggesting that maybe on a subconscious level, it had something to do with feelings of abandonment she had with her father, and a fear that men who gave her love were destined to take it back—unless she took it back first, which she always made sure to do. She seemed to appreciate the perspective.

We moved to the couch and spent a half hour analyzing texts from her most recent crush. I became frustrated, impatient, and took her by the face. "My God, you're so caught up in your own head," I said. "This isn't … *living*." I pointed to the park through her window. "Do you ever just go to the park, feel the grass beneath your feet, and look up at the sky?" I was playing the role of sage, but it felt more real than the days when I regurgitated clichés on our porch.

We went outside to walk her dog and watched it bounce from bush to bush. Again, I was reminded of *The Painted Veil*, the contrast between Kitty Fane at the beginning and the end of the movie. By the end of the story, Kitty had achieved a level of maturity, mental calmness, and dignity. To me, she had become beautiful. I wondered if Jade would ever get there. It was my wish for her.

Around two o'clock in the morning, I stumbled to the couch. Peering into the kitchen, I watched Jade knock down a shot of vodka. She slid onto the couch beside me, feet to head. We rambled and laughed. Then the kissing started. In two years of knowing each other, which included a year of living together, we'd never once been intimate. Now we were giving each other sensations. It lasted a couple of minutes before we stopped and reminded ourselves that we were friends—and friends aren't supposed to give each other sensations. No big deal. It happens. We moved past it.

But Jade began drinking more. She had more flings. More sadness. And then she disappeared. My texts went unanswered and my calls went to voicemail. I got that feeling in my stomach. Jade had always considered modern life insufferable, so much so that she welcomed a freak catastrophic accident into her life, because it would free her from this cruel, responsibility-filled world. Had she gotten the accident she had always desired? Or had she taken matters into her own hands? I called her mother.

"We're in Colorado," she said. "At a treatment center for depression."

I was relieved to hear that Jade was okay. I told her mother I thought her daughter was brave for seeking treatment and that I was proud of her. I said I'd be there for Jade on the other side. When she returned from Colorado a month later, we had dinner that weekend on an outside patio at a restaurant in Back Bay. It was a warm summer evening.

I asked her what happened. Jade told me that she had gone to a dark place—the wine, the flings, and one man had been too forceful. But she was feeling better. Her job had been discontinued in her absence, but she'd already scheduled an interview for a new job with higher pay and managerial responsibilities. She bought a keyboard and liked to play Beethoven. She attended spin classes twice a week and looked slimmer and more athletic. She was also in the process of reconciling with her first boyfriend, having visited him in Utah to try and mend the wounds he had unwittingly left.

When we got back to her apartment, Jade played Für Elise for me on her keyboard. After, we sprawled out on the couch, and unexpectedly gave each other a new type of sensations. We played The Love Game.

Jade brought up the last night we had seen each other before she went away. "I remembered you said I should look into the real reasons my relationships fail, directing my attention to my father. That became the focus of my work in Arizona." She said she never considered how her father had impacted every relationship she'd had. "Your insight started me in the direction of doing the real reflecting I've always needed to do."

Reciprocating the gratitude, I thanked her for pushing me during our sessions on the porch. I told her the cathartic nature of The Hate Game was likely the reason I had sought out therapy, and both had given me a better perspective on myself. While I still dropped the occasional platitude from my readings, I thought I was less clichéd and pedantic. I didn't take myself as seriously as I once had. It was also quite possible that, because of her, I had become more capable of compassion, a far cry from the days of pretending I didn't know anything about sadness or loneliness.

"And maybe I helped you realize what a brilliant friend you are," she said. I was thinking the same thing about her. "It's because of friends like you that struggling people can hold on to hope," she continued. "You showed me that I don't have to feel so alone. And that is the best thing in this world."

It's been years since I played The Hate Game, but I always try and remember its purpose: to point out the bigger issues within ourselves. Jade and I live in different cities now and haven't spoken in a long time, but I always like to think of her walking her dog in a park and kneeling down to squeeze its squirming face. The next time we see each other, I hope to walk in a park together. There, we can look at the sky, feel the grass beneath our feet, and play The Hate Game, with love.

CHAPTER 8

Departing Down the Middle

In the movies, when someone leaves for an extended period of time, their significant other drives to a quiet park outside the airport. There, they sit on a bench and spot their loved one's plane as it lifts off, watching it fly away until it disappears.

In the real world, you drop off your girlfriend, slump down in the driver's seat, misty-eyed and melancholy, and then merge into traffic behind a shuttle with *Love the Journey* written on the back.

In Sanskrit, the word *taṇhā* means "thirst," another word for desire—the clinging to objects, people, and even identities, which, if not balanced, can cause headaches and heartaches. Buddhists use the word to mean "suffering"—a fire that burns hot when we can't let go of something but smolders quietly when we come to terms with the supreme natural law: that nothing lasts and change is constant.

As we drove into the airport, I saw the split ahead: *Arrivals* and *Departures*. For a moment, I indulged in a fantasy: I would turn into the arrivals area and park my car with the hazards flashing. From the driver's seat, I'd spot my girlfriend Paige, duffel bag on her shoulder and head on a swivel. However, as I turned my car toward Departures, the fantasy evaporated. As appealing as it was—as much as I would have liked Paige to be arriving, not departing—I had to accept reality: this day was about goodbyes.

It was a good lesson in attachment, I suppose. She left, I stayed, and we were all supposed to be okay with it. As I drove into the terminal, I wondered how a Buddhist might act in such a situation. When the car stopped, would he spring out happily and merrily send his loved one off, even though the length of her stay was indefinite, certainly longer than a year? Would this Buddhist remain ambivalent, his emotions on an even keel—not too hot, not too cold?

It's hard for me to imagine anyone being emotionally detached in such a situation. I'd like to think that even a Buddhist, open to the painful moment, would cry. It would be an honest response, a human reaction. As this Buddhist held his loved one close, he might tell her he was proud of her, as I did. Perhaps he'd say he would miss her deeply, as I did. Then he would use his sleeve to wipe his damp eyes and remind himself, as she walked away, that life isn't all about arrivals; it's made up of a lot of departures too.

We all have our fair share of departures. As painful as they are, the healthy response seems to involve feeling them honestly and completely. Then, though easier said than done, let them go. Leave the pain at the airport, so to speak.

Of course, those feelings will spring up now and again. Maybe when you roll over in bed and remember the first time you shared "I love yous." Or perhaps in the car, when you hear the song you belted together on that one road trip. I suppose a Buddhist would advise letting the memory pass through you. He'd likely caution against letting it hook you and take you for a ride.

As I drove home, following the shuttle with its ironic quip, I thought about attachment and how to achieve a balance when saying goodbye to the people we love. There's error, it seems, in being too loosely attached, using aloofness as a coping mechanism. Equally unhealthy would be letting oneself be crippled by emotion.

There's a teaching from the Buddha, a story he told his disciples: "Fair goes the dancing when the sitar is tuned." A string too tight will break, and a string too slack has no sound. With either, the music dies. However, there is a middle way: "Tune us the sitar neither low nor high, and we will dance away the hearts of men."

Such is a metaphor for life, discovering that healthy balance with the objects and, most especially, the people we desire. As I paid the toll and drove away from the airport, I made my own departure—down the middle.

PART II

Departed

2015–2018

To venture causes anxiety, but not to venture is to lose one's self…. And to venture in the highest is precisely to be conscious of one's self.

—Søren Kierkegaard

CHAPTER 9

In Defense of Quixote

According to *Merriam-Webster*, the word *quixotic* means "foolishly impractical, especially in the pursuit of ideals … marked by rash, lofty, romantic ideas or extravagantly chivalrous action." The word originated from the literary character Don Quixote, the hero of Miguel de Cervantes's novel about a middle-aged squire who suffers a nervous breakdown, changes his name, and embarks on a quest to slay giants, sack castles, and win the heart of a beautiful maiden. The only problem is, his quest is a fiction: The giants are windmills. The castle's inhabitants are village folk, not adversaries. And his lady fair? A figment of his overactive imagination.

I was first introduced to the word *quixotic* when reading about the death of Dean Potter, the extreme athlete and mountain climber who died in 2015 in a wingsuit accident. Potter stood for the ultimate form of living: cheating death. I've always admired extreme athletes, in particular, Alex Honnold, a legendary climber who often scales cliff faces without ropes, a controversial technique known as "free soloing." A few weeks after Potter's death, Honnold published an article in *Time* magazine in which he extolled Potter's perspective on life, referring to his pursuits as "quixotic."

The day after I read the article, a friend who was visiting from out of town pulled from his duffel bag a copy of *Don Quixote*. It was his go-to read whenever he was in a time of transition, which he certainly was then. He'd just gotten out of graduate school and was jobless but hopeful.

As my friend explained this, it struck me that I, too, was in transition. I was planning to quit my job and embark on an epic year-long adventure of traveling and writing.

I used to be more quixotic but working in offices had left me timid—downright docile even, at times. Part of the issue was the role of a staff writer in business settings. A hired gun is subject to committees and perfunctory analyses.

"The article is just—I don't know—too long," a project manager might say after reading an article I'd written for the company. "Can you get it down to a thousand words?"

"Can you end the article with a question?" a marketing executive might add. "More people will comment if it has a question at the end."

In today's "conceptual age," businesses like to tell magazines like *Inc.* that they want creative types: employees with big ideas, high emotional intelligence, and technological savvy—right- and left-brainers. On paper, they are godsends to capitalism, and managers ask them to supply ideas.

What most business leaders don't realize, or refuse to acknowledge, is that "good" ideas are path-breaking, oftentimes irreverent and impractical. The once-coveted employees are quickly perceived as idealistic, cavalier, too honest, perhaps impulsive, romantic, and even crass or impolitic.

Employers forget that the same imagination that generates good ideas has little interest in politics, often questions authority, and seeks reformation—all of which can undermine an institution's rules or defy departmental standards. Ask enough questions, and bosses start to wonder if they've hired a troublemaker. Inquisitive personnel soon realize that if they keep rocking the ship, they'll get thrown overboard.

And I was, once.

After that, I decided to bite my tongue in office settings, be more diplomatic. I drove my ideas into computer screens: novels, articles, and essays. But I could no longer ignore the gravitational pull of writing on my own terms and focusing on a medium I'd come to learn was aligned with some of my natural abilities: screenwriting. Deciding to go for broke, I spent six months planning my escape from my job to hopefully become a writer in the movie industry.

As you can imagine, doubt crept in, and uncertainty took hold. Whenever I considered the practical implications, I would second-guess myself. I began to see *Don Quixote* as a mirror. Was I moving toward self-actualization or tilting at windmills? Did I move to Los Angeles (of all places) to find myself or lose myself? Did I actually want what I wanted, or was I just in love with *wanting*?

On a whim, I reached out to Dr. Matthew Schneider, an English professor at North Carolina's High Point University. Dr. Schneider had written an article entitled "Howard Hughes and Don Quixote" that had resonated with me. I thought he might be able to comment on my situation and the idea of transitioning through the lens of Cervantes's book.

"*Don Quixote* is timelessly entertaining," Dr. Schneider said over the phone. "Cervantes was a masterful storyteller, so it works as a book, but the deeper resonance captured an aspect of human nature that might never change. It dramatizes this conflict between our sense of selves—who and what we think we are—and what we can get society to believe about us."

Dr. Schneider offered an example. "Imagine someone who considers themselves a 'people-person.' This individual believes they get along with everybody, that they're persuasive and friendly in their dealings. But the world isn't interested in acknowledging them as a people-person. So implicitly or explicitly, in a thousand ways, the world delivers its feedback: *You? No, no—you're not a people-person. In fact, you're not who you think you are.*"

"Personal and career transitions, especially, can trigger such feedback because you're announcing to the world that you're going to be this 'other' person now."

Persisting in the face of such resistance takes self-determination, which Dr. Schneider defined as the "freedom to live as one chooses or to act or decide without consulting others."

In other words, deciding who you are and what you want to be.

Don Quixote was a champion of self-determination. I couldn't help but admire him for his conviction. But I also pitied him when he sold his farmland and let his house go to ruin while he devoured novels about romantic chivalry.

When Quixote leaves on his quest and arrives at a guesthouse, he mistakes it for a castle. He finds the innkeeper as "governor" of the castle and two prostitutes as "ladies of the game." At first, the village folk are confused, but seeing Quixote's conviction, they start treating him like the knight he believes he is and talk with him in the terms of his world. Indulging Quixote's self-delusion, the innkeeper recites a hymn, as if Quixote were a knight, and the prostitutes perform the parts of fair maidens.

As a character, this is Quixote's charm and fatal flaw. He seems to proclaim: *I am who I choose to be. So what if it's fake?*

"Don Quixote chose a different—and fictional—persona," Dr. Schneider continued. "Through the sheer force of his self-belief, he got the world to adopt a standard of living, a mode of address, and even a way of acting." Quixote showed that when you're transitioning or assuming a new identity, a strong conviction, even self-delusion, can go a long way. If you believe in the lie enough, sometimes the world just accepts the identity you've chosen.

Most of us can think of someone like this. They're the "crazy" ones. Let's call them *Quixotes*. Through sheer will and self-belief, they get us to see the world through their eyes and even believe their fantasies. Perhaps like two bicycle mechanics from Ohio who dreamed that man could fly like the birds and now airships fly between continents. Sixty years after the Wright brothers first flew an airplane, humans blasted a rocket ship into space and left footprints on the moon.

In Dr. Schneider's article, he described how the film *The Aviator* portrayed Howard Hughes as quintessentially quixotic: "Impetuous, impractical, eager to sink his wealth and prodigious energies into extravagant projects, like commissioning the largest airplane the world had ever seen."

Whether they work in business or science, engineering or law, Quixotes are people on quests. They show relentless drive, wild curiosity, and original vision. But their genius is their unflinching belief in themselves.

"*The Aviator* touchingly portrays Hughes—damaged psyche and all—asserting his quixotic right of self-determination with bracing valor," Dr. Schneider wrote. In other words, he proclaimed, "This is who I am. *Deal with it.*"

A Quixote to the stars is Elon Musk, an entrepreneur, engineer, inventor, and investor. Musk gave the world PayPal, SpaceX, Tesla, and SolarCity. In the opening of a published biography, *Elon Musk: Tesla, SpaceX, and the Quest for a Fantastic Future*, Ashlee Vance described his first meeting with Musk. Over dinner, Musk asked, "Do you think I'm insane?"

It's a legitimate question. Don't quixotic folks like Musk always flirt with that knife's edge between rationality and insanity? What's wonderful about Musk is that he's aware of his self-delusional abilities. He knows he's a little nuts. That's what separates Musk from Don Quixote, who actually thought he was battling giants instead of windmills.

"The key to quixotic thinking is not stopping in the face of obstacles," Dr. Schneider said. "It's holding onto your vision when everyone tells you to give it up."

As a writer, I just want to tell stories. True stories, invented stories. Big ones, small ones, meaningful ones, absurd ones. Isn't it just a tad quixotic to think your ideas and stories can change minds and influence culture? That your literary inventions hold truths that others can't see? To nourish the utopian idea of artistic freedom—to write what you want, when you want, and get paid for it?

Perhaps my doubt was the result of not having convinced myself yet. I was being rather prudent, having decided to leave my job nine months out. I then spent several months preparing first for a three-week trip in China and then buying supplies for a motorcycle journey across the country, putting off the moment I would break the news to my employer.

When I worked up the courage to tell my boss, I told her I'd recently applied to an MFA program in screenwriting. The senior admissions officer had told me that the writing department had reviewed my creative work, and I apparently didn't need the program. I should just go to Los Angeles and try to break into the movie industry. Because I had "talent," he had added.

My boss understood. More importantly, she saw my conviction.

It was the right decision for me because I'd convinced myself first. No longer was I languishing in self-doubt, wondering if this was a mistake. I had achieved self-determination. Several years in offices had beaten me up, but I was still quixotic at heart. Like the time I'd bought a plane ticket to East Africa and then told my boss at the time that I was leaving for two weeks to hike Mount Kilimanjaro. Or when I applied to a Ph.D. program without considering that I was committing the next five years of my life.

Or when I drove across the country and back in an unreliable car at a time when gas prices were the highest they had been in years. Or when I signed up for a skydiving certification class because I loved the movie *Point Break*. Or when I bought a motorcycle after reading *Zen and the Art of Motorcycle Maintenance*. Or engaging in a series of long-term relationships in pursuit of the "perfect love" that didn't exist.

Yet in all these examples, like most Quixotes, I was out of touch. I underestimated (okay, disregarded) the elevation of Kilimanjaro and suffered from altitude sickness. Six months into the graduate program, I switched from a Ph.D. to a master's when I realized that what I wanted was not to do or teach science but write about it instead. While driving across the country, my car's brakes wore down, and the electric engine fan broke, causing the radiator to overheat several times. As for the skydiving certification? When I didn't jump the first day due to high winds, I never returned. And the motorcycle? I drove it once and then didn't touch it for a year.

The common thread: Fantasy is better than reality.

Yet this craving for utopia seems universal. Don't we all have a little trouble being content? Don't we seem programmed to want something "better"? Dr. Schneider evoked the playwright Lord Bryon, who believed we are "half dust, half deity." That is, humans live in two worlds: the world of the material and the world of the imagination. We are physical creatures, bound by natural laws such as gravity, the inevitable decay of matter, and death—Byron's "half dust." Yet even as these natural forces work against us, we push back against them through imagination and aspirations—"half deity."

"In 1903, human-powered flight wasn't considered possible," Dr. Schneider wrote in his article. "But something about the human spirit longed to defy gravity. We weren't built to fly, but a few had the dream and set out to do it."

Most of the time, we're comfortable listening to the half-dust part of our psyches. It's the "sane" thing. But we should remind ourselves of the half-deity part of human nature; "insanity" is built into our DNA. It's our madness and our genius. Our charm and our fundamental flaw.

In my time of transition, I entertained both parts. I acknowledged the dust but embraced the deity. I acted from the spirit but stayed grounded in facts. I took the middle ground between realistic cynic and Pollyanna dreamer.

If I had to pick just one part, though, I'd choose deity. I'd choose self-determination. Because if Quixote and other dreamers have taught us anything, it's that reality becomes what you believe.

Am I insane? Perhaps.

But you'll see it my way, eventually.

CHAPTER 10

Finding My Sleep in China

The traditional Chinese doctor took my right hand and pressed three fingers against the radial artery on my wrist. I took a deep breath as she titled her head downward to concentrate on my pulse.

"Do you have a sore throat?" my guide translated for the doctor.

I shook my head.

The doctor focused again. Then she spoke to my guide for several minutes, making me feel left out of my own diagnosis, not to mention fear the worse.

My guide, a warm-hearted Chinese man in his mid-thirties, turned to me and delivered the diagnosis. "She says you have too much fire." I touched my forehead, not feeling hot. "A fever?" I asked. More talking in Chinese. They began laughing, and I forced a smile. "No, no—the doctor says the fire might be from being in a new country."

But it wasn't culture shock. I was stressed because I had just quit my job to carry out a rejected Fulbright/National Geographic Digital Storytelling fellowship, a project that focused on Traditional Chinese Medicine (TCM), which included a broad range of 2,000-year-old medical practices, such as acupuncture, Tui Na massage, tai chi and qigong, dietary therapy, and herbal medicine.

And so, I couldn't sleep.

My first night in Beijing, I awoke at 3:45 a.m. When I woke up the next morning at 4:00 a.m., I tiptoed into my hostel's common area, surprised to see a young Chinese girl clicking through webpages at the front desk.

"Why are you working so early?" I asked.

She rubbed her eyes. "I lost my sleep."

I had also lost my sleep, and I hoped it would come back soon.

I went looking for my sleep with Ziming, a medicinal chemist at my Fulbright application's host institution, the Institute for Materia Medica in Beijing. Our first stop was Tongrentang, a traditional herbal pharmacy founded in 1669. Ziming led me through the front doors, past pharmacists in white coats standing behind glass counters, packing bags with herbal remedies for Chinese suffering from minor health issues, such as a fever, headache, or cold. Tongrentang is the largest producer of Traditional Chinese Medicine in the country. The interior resembles an American CVS, though instead of melatonin and hand sanitizers on the shelves, there are oddly shaped plants and herbs and alien-looking animal parts. Known for their medicinal properties, the twisted roots and mushrooms, antlers and horns, ants and scorpions emit potent smells, ranging from pleasant swirls of ginger to pungent aromas of decaying material.

There are over 13,000 medicinal substances used in China and over 100,000 herbal recipes recorded in the ancient literature. I told Ziming about my insomnia and suggested we look for an energy elixir. He led me up the stairs, and we stopped at a shelf of Ginseng, an herb that looked like pumpkin seeds.

"Good for energy, but expensive," Ziming said.

I converted the price—$150 Yuen was twenty-three American dollars—which seemed reasonable.

"Something else?" Ziming offered.

"Any herbal medicines for sleep?"

It was quite American of me—something to bring me up, something to bring me down, but Ziming didn't think twice and led me to the first floor, where he exchanged rapid-fire conversation with a pharmacist and then flipped through a notebook with lists of traditional drugs. The pharmacist traced her finger to a string of Chinese characters. "Tongren Anshen Wan," Ziming translated. "A calming agent." The woman behind the counter retrieved a rectangular yellow box that contained eight small balls, each composed of ten medicinal Chinese herbs that were supposed to relax the body by "nourishing the blood" and "boosting Qi." Qi translates as "breath" or "air" but figuratively represents the body's "life force."

I reached for my wallet, but the pharmacist shook her head.

"You need a prescription from a traditional Chinese doctor," Ziming said.

"Can I get an appointment?"

Ziming wasn't sure, but he spoke with the receptionist in the waiting room next to the pharmacy. She told him that I needed an ailment ... and money.

"Insomnia," I said, handing the receptionist 100 Yuen (fifteen dollars).

She hesitated, then printed a ticket for me. We sat on a bench outside the doctor's office, which was concealed by a thick red curtain. On the wall beside the curtain was a plaque with a headshot of the traditional doctor, a middle-aged woman wearing a firm expression, black rectangular glasses, and tightly pulled-back hair. The curtain moved aside, and an elderly man stepped out, holding his prescription on a sheet of paper.

Ziming peeked into the room and then waved me over.

The interior didn't have the typically sterile feel of an American doctor's office. Tucked in the corner was a charming granite sink with gold fixtures and flowers etched on the side. Above a bureau in the back was a cabinet with a black-and-white photograph of a Chinese pagoda painted on the glass. The doctor was seated at a mahogany desk across from an eager apprentice. Ziming briefed the doctor in Chinese, telling her that I was a writer who was interested in her craft, one who'd also slept less than eight hours since arriving.

The doctor smiled warmly. I relaxed, feeling the urge to leave a comment card after the session to say that the doctor's serious-looking headshot hardly reflected her pleasant bedside manner. The examination began. The doctor looked me over to get an impression of my exterior, as it held clues to my interior. She pointed to my mouth.

"Stick out your tongue," Ziming said.

Ziming explained that a healthy tongue is pink, flat, and wet. If I had a cold, for instance, the doctor would observe a pale tongue, spotted with red dots and teeth marks at the edges. She inspected my tongue and nodded with approval.

It was then that she examined my pulse and told me that I had "too much fire," a diagnosis that I didn't understand. But Traditional Chinese Medicine can be unintelligible like that, even for the Chinese. Flummoxed himself, Ziming later consulted a traditional doctor on my behalf. In an email, he wrote that the "fire" likely referred to "internal heat." There's "good" fire that provides strength and energy, but also "bad" fire associated with inflammation. Fire was also figurative. "A man with a big fire" could symbolize an angry or spirited man, whereas "a man with a small fire" might represent a timid or meek one.

Ziming presented the Ginseng I'd bought to the doctor. She turned the bag around in her hands and chuckled. Ziming explained the humor. Most herbal medications are imported from Asia, but my Ginseng was sourced from the United States, and it amused her that I'd be bringing it back home. Then she explained that it wasn't wise that a man with too much fire would soon be supplementing with a stimulant.

"Wait until winter before you take this—when it's colder," Ziming said.

And I'd calmed down, I presumed.

The doctor's face brightened when Ziming presented the Tongren Anshen Wan, which, I learned, wasn't principally a sleep agent. It was more like an anti-anxiety medication, prescribed to "quiet the spirit," Ziming explained.

Just what the doctor ordered, I thought.

The doctor scribbled a prescription on her notepad and handed the page to me.

After the appointment, Ziming and I took a taxi to the Hospital of Acupuncture of Moxibustion. A traditional doctor and acupuncturist met us in the hallway, wearing a white coat and dark-rimmed glasses. He led us to a secluded section of the hospital where he was caring for four patients lying in beds, each undergoing traditional Chinese treatments.

The doctor lifted his chin toward an empty bed.

"He's asking if you would like to try," Ziming said. I glanced at the acupuncture needles stuck in patients' limbs and the smoke rising from incense-like tubes on their chests. They were routine treatments, according to my guide, but they looked invasive, and I wasn't exactly eager to go under the knife. But a man will do just about anything for a good night's rest, so I climbed into the bed.

Knowing I was having trouble sleeping, the doctor retrieved acupuncture needles from a stainless-steel cart. "Good for poor sleep," he said and then tapped a needle into the crown of my scalp. It was unexpected but perhaps only as unpleasant as the needle prick experienced when giving blood. The doctor moved around my body mechanically, placing two needles on each side of my neck, two in each wrist, and two in each ankle.

"Fifteen minutes," Ziming said. He explained that the needles stimulated the meridian system, a complex network of psychic channels through which Qi flows. The procedure wasn't especially painful, more disconcerting, particularly when the doctor repositioned a needle deeper in my wrist; I had to keep my arm absolutely still, less I would drag tiny tendons against the steel.

Following acupuncture, I underwent a procedure known as Scrape Therapy. I removed my shirt and sat at the edge of the bed. The doctor vigorously scraped my upper back with a comb-like tool. Supposedly, the treatment helped clear toxins from my body by stimulating blood flow.

"Scrape therapy also relaxes the cervical vertebrae, which are often stiff from sitting at a desk for long periods," Ziming said, translating for the doctor.

It was a rather hostile procedure made even more distressing after the doctor tilted a hand-held mirror so I could see my back, which had become a battlefield of bright red streaks.

"The redness should go away in three-to-four days," Ziming assured me. "But please call me if they don't."

The doctor instructed me to flip onto my stomach for the next treatment, known as Cupping. He rolled over a cart holding six palm-sized glass cups. One at a time, he brought a cup near my upper back, positioned a lit match at the cup's opening to remove the oxygen, and then quickly inverted it onto my skin. Each cup created a tight seal, drawing my skin upward.

"It's meant to mobilize blood and energy," Ziming said. It was the first relaxing procedure, so I closed my eyes for the next ten minutes until the doctor popped off the cups, leaving behind dark red circular welts.

For the fourth procedure, called Moxibustion, the doctor fetched two cigar-shaped cylinders and erected them near my belly button. He used a match to ignite the cylinders' contents known as moxa, a flammable substance from a dried plant, typically mugwort, which is used medicinally in Asia. The heat, which at times became searing, was a method for stimulating blood flow by warming a region of the body.

"When applied to the stomach, it can help soothe constipation and ease digestion," Ziming said.

This time, the procedure hadn't scarred my body.

I was pleased to learn that the final treatment was Tui Na massage, which is "extremely good for a tired body and spirit," Ziming translated. The doctor performed unfamiliar massage techniques, including the rolling method, where he flipped his hand repeatedly along my lower back that sent tremors through my whole body and helped melt the tension in tight spots.

That afternoon, Ziming and I parted ways, and I took a train to Xi'an in Central China. As I traded the city's claustrophobic alleyways for the countryside, I felt more relaxed and began to forget the self-imposed duties of my writing project. At my hostel, I spent the extra money for a single room over the eight-person dormitory. As I unpacked, I opened the box of Tongren Anshen Wan. The balls inside were about ¾ inch in diameter. They looked like Whoppers, the malted milk balls made by The Hershey Company. I bit into one. It tasted bland until I broke through the thin chocolate shell and arrived at the bitter cocktail of herbs. My nose wrinkled, and I had to force myself to swallow. Thirty minutes later, I may have felt calmer, but the medicine's effects were imperceptible. Nevertheless, I slept deeply and soundly through the night.

Perhaps the fire was out, I thought.

Several days later, I continued southwest by train to the Yunnan province. The redness on my back was fading, along with my sleep issues. I arrived in Shangri-La, where I made the pilgrimage to the 300-year-old Ganden Sumtseling Gompa Tibetan monastery. The high altitude had the effect of sharpening my mind and calming my body.

As I strolled past Tibetan monks, I thought of my last conversation with Ziming. We had walked the streets following our meeting with the traditional Chinese doctor at Tongrentang, discussing my diagnosis of "too much fire." The doctor had detected some obvious stress and fatigue, but she had also put her finger on an existential ailment. Ziming referred to it as "a young's man condition." Not anger or insomnia, but passion, which burned hot with energetic dreams.

As we strolled, I told Ziming I was glad my fire still burned bright and grateful that someone had noticed its flames. I was thankful to have found my sleep, but I wasn't looking for a cure any time soon.

CHAPTER 11

Backed Up in China

It was my fourth day in Beijing without going number two.

That's four days of breakfast, lunch, dinner, some snacks, some drinks, all backed up and getting weird in thirty feet of cramped intestines. I had experienced backups in my travels, but ninety-six hours was ridiculous.

I was visiting China to study Traditional Chinese Medicine. I had intended to carry out the research via a Fulbright/National Geographic fellowship, but when my proposal didn't make the cut, I told my host advisor, Dr. Peicheng Zhang at the Institute for Materia Medica in Beijing, I was coming anyway.

By the second day in Beijing, I had adjusted to the deep stares my "blue eyes and yellow hair" were attracting, the city's frenetic pace, weaving mopeds and flashing stores with staff shouting discounts through headset microphones, but the food still vexed me. The dishes I was eating from curbside vendors were going in my body but not coming out, dropping into a seemingly bottomless pit of tangled noodles.

I was sightseeing when I felt those got-to-go pangs and scurried for a public bathroom. When I reached a stall, I fumbled with my belt and surveyed my surroundings. There was a sharp, foul odor and a glistening yellow stream at my feet, evidence of poor aim. Near the door was a cylindrical trash can topped off with dirty toilet paper. The plumbing in China isn't robust enough to transport paper, so you don't flush it, you store it—with everyone else's. I eyed the trash can and imagined what creatures were bedding down in its filthy ecosystem: parasites, bacteria, Velociraptors.

No, I thought. There will be no pooping today.

You might think my intestines sent side-splitting pain signals to my brain, forcing a bowel movement despite my mind's resistance. Perhaps there was a gaseous ejection, a shot across the bow, if you will? Maybe an accident?

No. My brain and bowels concurred.

And I held it.

With such Zen-like control over my colon, I predicted I could go days, maybe weeks, without defecating. I might never have to go again, I thought, and continued with my fellowship studies.

My Beijing guide was a soft-spoken medicinal chemist named Ziming, who met me at my hostel and taxied us to his lab at the Institute for Materia Medica. Waiting for us in Dr. Zhang's office were watermelon and grapes, which we munched on before Dr. Zhang, a quiet but brilliant man, joined us to discuss his lab's research that involved extracting and analyzing natural compounds from medicinal plants and herbs.

After the interview, the three of us joined other scientists at the communal ping pong table, where Ziming, paddle in hand, told me that he had read my Fulbright proposal and said he would be honored to take me to pharmacies, hospitals, institutes and universities that practiced or studied Traditional Chinese Medicine.

Later that night, the Zhang lab took me out to dinner for traditional Beijing cuisine. We used hot water to wash our chopsticks and plates, and then the table filled with white rice, vegetables, and various meats, followed by the main dish: succulent Peking duck. The meat was crispy on the outside, juicy on inside, and came with the warning, "Once bitten, forever smitten."

I spent the next two days crisscrossing Beijing with Ziming, visiting Tongrentang, a traditional herbal pharmacy, and then the Hospital of Acupuncture of Moxibustion, where I underwent acupuncture with a traditional doctor.

I said goodbye to the Zhang lab and was waiting for a train in a crowded terminal when I realized that my insides had become bunched up like the travelers around me vying for exits. I admitted that there was nothing Zen about my perceived control over my bowels. Like everyone else, I was a slave to the meals I had eaten forty-eight hours prior.

Truth be told, Nature had been calling all along, and I wasn't going because I was afraid: of the parasites, the bacteria, the raptors. I knew this constipation had to end, and the train station was my Waterloo.

I hustled into the station's bathroom, opened a stall door, and locked eyes with a Chinese man hovering over a squat toilet. He glanced up from his cell phone, a cigarette dangling from his lips, a blank expression on his face. Oops, sorry. The next stall was vacant, and I squeezed my forty-pound backpack into the narrow space.

I hung my pack on the door and frowned at the trash can next to me.

I took a deep breath and told myself there weren't prehistoric beasts scratching at the trash can's interior. I hovered over the squat toilet and reminded myself that the only poop to fear was poop itself. And I went.

A decidedly lighter human being, I took a seat on the train and watched the countryside rush by until I arrived five hours later in Xi'an in Central China. As I walked the city's Muslim Quarter, I thought about Chinese medicine, which is based on the notion of harmony and balance. I realized I'd been out of balance in Beijing—and backed up as a result. Perhaps it was jetlag, or the city's hectic pace, or the stress of the reporting duties I'd imposed on myself as a writer. Either way, I was intent on regaining my balance and decided to avoid major cities for the next two weeks. I continued south by train, trading the city's congested alleyways for the wide-open spaces of the Yunnan Province.

In China's Guangxi region, I avoided a bus from Guilin to Yangshuo, opting instead to float down the Li River on a bamboo raft. On the shuttle bus to the river, a young Chinese woman tapped me on the shoulder. She introduced herself as Jenny and said she was a third-year college student from the Guangdong province. We became fast friends, chatting through slow, choppy English. We decided to share a bamboo raft and gazed in awe at the breathtaking karst peaks hugging the tranquil Li River.

From the raft, Jenny and I watched fishermen snag fish with cormorants. We took pictures atop the 600-year-old Dragon Bridge. Later, we spent the evening strolling through the buzzing streets of Yangshuo. My stomach grumbled as restaurant staff hounded us along walkways, pointing at laminated menus displaying main courses of fish stews brewed in spices and vegetables.

Jenny turned to me and smiled. "Maybe we take a table?"

CHAPTER 12

Walkabout Love

A Chinese teenager with puffed cheeks sprang from the seat beside me, begged a man for his lunch bag, and filled it with peach-colored vomit. The driver stopped the bus at a roadside store. I bought the girl a Ginger Ale to tame her stomach and then slumped into my seat as the bus roared alive and continued along switchbacks toward Lijiang in northwest China.

I'd recently ended a four-year-long relationship with a woman I've been calling Paige and was hoping for solitude during my three-week trip through China. I was prepared for long stretches of alone time, even bouts of loneliness. My trip hadn't turned out that way. As I watched limestone cliffs pass through my window, I thought about a Chinese woman who was now just a memory.

I had met Jenny four days earlier on a shuttle bus in Guilin in Southeast China. We were both headed to the Li River for a bamboo raft ride. As we left the shuttle and walked toward the water, she told me she'd never been on a boat and couldn't swim.

Jenny was a third-year college student with long black hair that hugged a sweet, slender face. She had a gentle way about her, a kind and innocent soul. She told me she'd wanted to visit the Li River ever since writing an essay about its waters in the fifth grade. "It makes a woman's skin more beautiful," she said.

The region of China had a mystical, old-world mood. It wasn't difficult to see why it had attracted artists, poets, and seekers for centuries. As we snaked down the river, we passed colossal limestone hills with mist swirling around knife-edged cliffs. From the ancient, stone-arched Dragon Bridge, we watched anglers use cormorants to catch fish.

On the bus back to Yangshuo, we talked about relationships. "I'm not willing to take a boyfriend casually," Jenny said, admitting that she had never kissed a boy. She wanted to wait for her first kiss from her first serious boyfriend.

As the shuttle pulled into town, we retrieved our bags and came in close for what I thought would be a goodbye hug. Instead, I learned she had changed plans and decided to stay at my hostel. She asked if I had plans for the evening. I'd battled food poisoning the night before and was exhausted, but I agreed. I liked spending time with her.

As we explored the streets of Yangshuo, searching for a table, I sensed something romantic stirring between us. Throughout the day, Jenny and I found subtle, polite ways of making contact. She took my hand and led me into a shop to show me a flute she had played in school. I placed a hand gently on her back as we crossed a street.

We chose a restaurant, and Jenny showed me how to use hot water to wash our chopsticks and plates. White rice and vegetables were then served, followed by the main course, a delicious stew of fish, spices, and vegetables.

As we ate, I explained my desire for a radical life change. I told Jenny I'd broken away from Corporate America and had flown to China to travel and write. I explained that when I returned home, I was planning to spend some time at my father's house in New Hampshire, and then I would ride my motorcycle to Southern California, where I would support myself on freelance writing. I confessed that my whole plan might fail spectacularly, but I figured I'd learn some things, either way.

Still a college student, Jenny hadn't yet worked a "real job," so I got the sense she couldn't fully understand the ennui that could accompany the workaday. Nonetheless, she admired my decision to split from the workforce and blaze a different path for myself.

"Not everyone has the courage to give up a comfortable life," she said, "but you've been searching for what you want and always fighting for it."

Later that night, we hugged tenderly and retreated to separate rooms. The next morning, I joined Jenny for a day trip to Silver Cave, which featured a mile and a half of crystal stalactites and calcites. After our tour, we strolled to Jenny's hostel, pausing on the front steps to say our goodbyes.

"When will I see you again?" Jenny asked somberly.

I was leaving for another town in a few hours. "We probably won't see each other again," I confessed, "but I'm really glad to have met you."

Walkabout Love

We hugged and I left for the bus station.

I found myself not wanting to hug Jenny, but to hold her. I felt like jumping off my bus before it left town to tell her how I felt.

Jenny was also smitten and messaged me through WeChat.

"When we separated, I didn't know why my heart hurt," she wrote. "It was the first time I had this kind of feeling."

She posted a picture of our bamboo ride to WeChat's newsfeed. It was an image of our shoes side-by-side. The caption read: "Meeting was a beautiful thing, but the worst is to leave. Thank you for giving me the most happy and impressive memory."

Several days later, a mile into a hike in Tiger Leaping Gorge, over 12,000 feet deep in places, I met an English woman in her late thirties. Kathryn had a fit body, piercings in her nose and tongue, and short curly hair with swirls of gray. She was an intellectual and a free spirit. We got along famously.

Kathryn's job teaching English had taken her all over the world. Adventurous and brave, she'd gone on motorcycle rides across Europe and was in China on a walkabout, this time without her bike.

The idea of a walkabout piqued my interest. A "walkabout" is an Australian rite of passage where a young man enters the wilderness alone to make the spiritual journey into manhood. Had I not crossed paths with Kathryn, I might not have fully realized the reasons I left home. I wasn't just grieving a lost relationship; I was on a quest exploring myself, examining the questions I hadn't had time at home to explore.

Why am I here? How should I live? Who should I love?

Kathryn understood. Our conversation pivoted seamlessly from the philosophical to the absurd as we ambled through farming villages, paused at outlooks to marvel at glaciated peaks, sidestepped farmers nudging mountain goats down steep trails, and tiptoed around narrow bends that dropped off to terraced farmlands and a turquoise Jinsha River below.

We finished the hike in a speedy seven hours and made our way down a paved road to a guesthouse. Kathryn invited me to share a room, and we split the price.

After dinner, we tucked ourselves into separate beds and shared stories and laughed. After some silence, I could tell she was nearly asleep. I thought about Jenny and how I'd missed an opportunity to become intimate with someone I'd liked.

I took a chance. "I have a question," I said.

She flipped over to face me.

"Should we be … doing stuff?"

"What do you mean?"

"Like, hooking up?"

"Oh," she said, surprised. "That hadn't occurred to me."

It hadn't occurred to her?

"I was almost asleep, so I think I will drift off."

I felt silly, if not embarrassed. I'd misread the situation. She saw me as fellowship—friendly, a good listener, trustworthy. Becoming physical wasn't a priority.

Why had I tried to shoehorn a hook-up into a perfectly fine day? Drifting off to sleep, I reminded myself that I'd come to China in search of solitude, not romance. But I couldn't deny that something had changed since arriving in the country. My travel companions had made me rethink my trip's original intent.

There wasn't any awkwardness the next morning. We joked about the great "television show" playing through our window that gave us a majestic view of the side of a mountain. I told her that I had to catch a bus soon, so we went to get breakfast.

The coffee was strong, and our banter continued over eggs. We joked about my advance the night before. She hoped her rejection hadn't been too emasculating.

I said that I enjoyed her company and sharing a room had kept the good times alive. We cleaned our plates and exchanged email addresses.

On my flight home, I thought about how you sometimes find what you're not looking for. I'd traveled to China in search of solitude and had discovered—anew—the joys of companionship. I didn't realize it then, but my journey was the beginning of something enduring with Jenny.

We stayed in contact, exchanging texts and letters and speaking on the phone every few months. We shared selfies while working and relaxing. She liked to send Chinese songs and poems. Sometimes I'd quote authors and make book recommendations—*Walden* by Henry David Thoreau was her favorite.

Over the ensuing weeks, we shared our setbacks and triumphs, our perspectives and philosophies. She displayed an insatiable hunger for knowledge, an eagerness to master the English language, and impatience for personal growth.

Stoking the fires of affection with a 24-year-old Chinese college student felt a bit unconventional. There were 7,000 miles separating us. The notion of such a long-distance relationship, in miles and culture, was as unrealistic as a walkabout in modern-day American culture. But the months passed, and our connection grew.

"Life is exciting and colorful, but also complicated and lost," she wrote in an old-fashioned letter to me. Jenny knew I could work myself ragged and sometimes took life—and myself—too seriously, so she always reminded me to stay present.

"Today, remember to look up at the blue sky."

After a year of staying connected, our affection had grown deep.

Jenny suggested a visit to the United States for a walkabout of her own. She began navigating China's thorny application process for an American visa. We prepared ourselves for the fact that it wouldn't happen.

"It is night in my land," she wrote on the eve of her interview at the U.S. embassy. "I will dream that I have gone to America to be with you."

Jenny texted me that morning as she walked into the embassy. A few hours later, she sent me a message: "Dustin, I just finished the interview. I got the visa!"

Days later, Jenny bought a plane ticket for a week-long trip to Boston in the fall.

When she arrives, I plan to continue the journey we began in China. We'll walk Boston's Freedom Trail and eat Italian food in the North End. I'll drive her south to Cape Cod and maybe ride the ferry to Martha's Vineyard.

And, of course, I plan to take her to Walden Pond. We'll walk the path around the pond to visit the site of Thoreau's one-room cabin in the woods. After, we can find a restaurant in Concord and take a table.

"I never found the companion that was so companionable as solitude," Thoreau wrote in *Walden*. Solitude suited Thoreau.

It does not, I learned, suit me.

CHAPTER 13

Letters from Dad

It was a chilly October morning when I passed the wooden sign for Kearsarge Cemetery in North Conway, New Hampshire. I walked the damp, narrow paths, brushing snow from headstones in search of my grandmother's name: Martha Anne Burke (who went by "Anne"). After a half hour, I turned toward the exit and texted my mother that I had come up empty. Talking to her from my father's house an hour before, I'd asked where her mother had been buried a decade ago. She gave me vague directions, unable to remember the exact location. While we were talking, I heard a loud thwack. A bird had flown into a window beside me. It died instantly, the third one in as many weeks.

My father's chalet is his own monastery. It's buried in the woods, tucked alongside a stream overlooking a small pond. It's the third house my father, Greg, has built on the unpaved road in Eaton Village, New Hampshire, a picturesque town in the White Mountains with a population of roughly 400 people. It's his empty nest, now that my brother and I are grown and living in Massachusetts. He calls it Shangri-La, a charming place to lay his head, if you ignore the intermittent thuds of beaks hitting glass.

The first time I witnessed a bird's fatal miscalculation, I was working on my laptop at the dining room table. I slid open the glass door and crept toward the stunned sparrow. The crown of its scalp was bloodied, eyes vacant. I watched the bird take its last puzzled breaths before its body went stiff. I buried it in the woods later that day.

I told my mother about the bird that had just flown into the window. "There's an old wives' tale about that," she said. "It means death is near."

I was about to visit a cemetery, and in a few weeks, I was planning to ride my motorcycle across the United States, so the timing was synchronous. I fancy myself a man of reason, not given to supernatural explanations for phenomena, but with a trip of such magnitude ahead of me, I could've done without the omen. My mother offered to visit the cemetery with me, but I insisted I go alone.

The graveyard was less than a mile from where my grandmother had lived most of her life. I had spent summers at Anne's house as a child, tinkering with tools in the backyard, among the rhythmic chirping of chickadees in the birch trees. Inside her home, I would sprawl out on the living room floor and send action figures on black-ops missions. Beside my play area was a cabinet full of decorative hummingbirds, which Anne collected. Every day, she would watch *The Price is Right* while making progress on a puzzle. In the afternoon, she would nap on the couch and "rest her eyes." The visits were escapes from the vortex of divorce. She died when I was seventeen, freezing those summer days in mental stasis.

There are many reasons for visiting a grave. Since I was moving across the country, perhaps I was visiting her grave to say goodbye. Maybe I wanted to tie up a loose end. I hoped it wasn't just a project. It was likely a result of my stay with my father, who is acutely aware of the brevity of this ride we call life. During the six weeks I lived with him before I left for California, he discussed a fatal diagnosis or mortal accident nearly every day.

"An old teacher of yours was diagnosed with brain cancer," he'd inform me during a commercial break while we watched the news. "A friend of mine is fighting for his life after a motorcycle accident," he said before he left for a ride of his own.

Fixating on death is Greg's way of illustrating his most cherished saying, cliché as it may be: *life is short*. Such insights usually came in the stillness of early morning, around 4 or 5 a.m. as he planned his workday over coffee. As I slept in the spare bedroom during my stay, he'd scribble reminders of life's shortness on scrap paper. I thought of these notes as letters—morning prayers, affirmations for his oldest son.

Some of these letters concerned mundane tasks. "Pick up some eggs, please," or "clean the stove after cooking." His standing order was: "leave no trace." But some letters offered deeper glimpses into his psyche, revealing thoughts we all share to a greater or lesser degree. "Most people don't think they could die tomorrow," one note said. "I don't think that way. Don't waste time. The world is your oyster."

Each day I awoke to his letters. "The next-door neighbor has cancer, won't see the spring. Fifty-five-years-old. Life is silly short, dude." Three weeks before I moved in, I was backpacking in China. Below a picture I had posted on Facebook of me hiking The Great Wall, my father wrote his favorite saying: "Geologically speaking, a human life is only ten seconds long."

An avid mountain biker, fierce downhill skier, and healthy eater, my father is the picture of health, but even at 59 years old, he suspects he's on borrowed time. When his father died at 55 and his uncle at 54, he began to think of the fifties as danger years. (It's worth noting that on the day I was born, he attended the funeral of his best friend's father.) Greg also thinks about the end because his mother won't stop talking about it.

While I was staying in Eaton, in Santa Barbara, California, his 77-year-old mother, Cheryl, was creating her living trust. Cheryl had made her son the executor and was inundating him with emails about his obligations upon her passing. He became frustrated. "I've just about had it with her emails," he said, snapping his laptop closed.

It made me realize that my father prefers to take a philosophical approach to death over his mother's more practical one. He also refuses to plan for death, because he's too busy getting the most out of life. Take a stroll around Shangri-La and life-affirming messages abound. Tacked to the walls or hanging in frames are postcards and pictures with inspirational quotes. A postcard in the downstairs bathroom has a mouse on the front wearing a helmet, inches from a block of cheese in a trap. Another quote hangs next to that, Hunter Thomson this time: "Life should not be a journey to the grave with the intention of arriving safely in a pretty and well-preserved body, but rather to skid in broadside in a cloud of smoke, thoroughly used up, totally worn out, and loudly proclaiming, 'Wow! What a ride!'"

A self-employed contractor, Greg spends his days replacing roofs and building additions or custom homes. If you call him in the morning, he'll tell you that he's "just building America." On the job site, you'll see a man working with a sense of urgency, eager for tangible measures of progress.

"We need a success," he once told me, as we stared at the foundation of a garage without walls. After we built and then stood up the walls, his mood brightened. He sang the lyrics to Tracy Chapman's "Fast Car" playing on the local radio station. During the commercial break, the station broadcasted its tagline—"93.5, music without boundaries"—to which he yelled in response: "No boundaries, baby!"

Greg's workdays end at 3:30 p.m., which justifies a fifteen-minute lunch. "Anything longer breaks momentum," he claims. When he gets home, he might call a friend and ask, "Can you play today?" An hour later, he'll be peddling his mountain bike up a stump-riddled trail, his heart rate jacked, eyes glued to the forest floor. Or perhaps he and his girlfriend might take a leisurely motorcycle ride on the Kancamagus Highway, a thirty-four-mile scenic highway that stretches from Conway to Lincoln, NH.

A week before my transcontinental journey, my brother Daniel and I were talking about our father as we walked the footpath around the Charles River in Boston. I pointed to a row of docks along the river.

"A year ago, I was having beers there with Dad and his girlfriend. I asked him who he thought the wisest person in our hometown was."

"What'd he say?" Daniel asked.

"He thought for a while but didn't have an answer." I paused, watching a sailboat bob on the Charles. "Honestly, I think Dad could make the shortlist."

At the time, I was reading *Meditations* by the Roman emperor Marcus Aurelius who repeatedly reminds the reader that death is inevitable. "Despise not death, but welcome it, for nature wills it like all else," wrote Aurelius.

It sounded like my father's letters.

As we strolled, my brother and I pondered our father's wisdom. We also balanced the "wise" with the not-so-wise—he was impatient, he could be judgmental, empathy wasn't always his strong suit, and his temper was the stuff of legend. However, despite his impatience and occasional intolerance, his lack of understanding and hotheadedness, he was something of a blue-collar mystic: Mount Washington Valley's philosopher king.

Daniel made a shrewd point: "Dad knows what's important."

He was referring to our father's parenting style. In that, during our childhood, he made it a priority to attend his kids' sporting events, reward good grades, and ensure our path to college, but he also continually reminded his boys that life is not to be wasted.

For thirty-three years, I had been on the receiving end of this wisdom, yet I had spent the last several years restless and disillusioned in office settings. I once promised myself that I would never inhabit a cubicle but broke that promise when I was promoted to the executive floor of a global company as a corporate communications writer.

On my first day in the new role, my boss walked me around the cubicle farm, passing offices for directors, vice presidents, and C-level executives.

"Pick any cubicle you want," she offered, as if it were a great honor to select a windowless box where I'd stare at a screen for eight hours a day, five days a week.

"It looks like a prison," I said.

She gave me a puzzled look. (Through experience, I learned not to speak in such ways among the institutionalized.)

At my next job, I had an office, but I still felt caged. Between meetings, I would gaze out my third-floor window into the busy square, my eyes flitting over pedestrians, like an eager puppy following hummingbirds at the feeder.

To decompress after work, I would visit the gym for a spin class, where I would bounce up and down for an hour, synchronizing to mashups and remixes. Later, I'd sprawl out on the couch and watch a movie or interviews with newsmakers.

It's difficult to complain, I guess. I had a stimulating job writing about science, in the stimulating city of Cambridge, at a stimulating workplace—a biomedical research institute, which some scientists likened to an artist's colony—but I was decidedly overstimulated. Intellectually, I was pleased with the life I had built, but my body was just along for the ride; I was living from the neck up. I feared if I didn't make a change, my body would rebel against my mind.

My father and I were eating dinner at the kitchen table when I brought up what seemed like his favorite subject.

"Are you afraid of death?" I asked.

His face contorted into a confused, almost defensive expression. "No, Dustin, I'm not afraid of death."

"Why do you talk about it so much?"

He took a sip of tequila. "I don't know."

I wondered if he was more afraid than average but had never admitted it to himself.

Unconsciously, I think we're all terrified of dying. We deny our own mortality because the concept of nonexistence is too difficult to bear. We go through lives as if we're not destined for old age, illness, and an inevitable death. We forget that everything is impermanent, nothing lasts, including ourselves.

I think discussing death is my father's way of dealing with this existential dread. It might be a subconscious way of nourishing the notion of impermanence, keeping it close so he wouldn't forget that any day could be our last. And in doing so, it would propel him to live a richer, fuller life.

"I'm afraid of dying," I told my father.

I didn't have a clear answer as to why. Part of it was that a human lifespan doesn't seem like enough time in my mind. I'm convinced I won't be able to say everything I need to say, learn everything I want to learn, do everything I hope to do in the 80 or so years I'm likely to live.

"I'm also not sure if anything happens when the lights go out," I added.

My father's reminders of death had certainly driven home the point that life was appallingly brief. But while I found his wisdom inspiring, I occasionally found it intimidating, if not paralyzing. Working a traditional nine-to-five job, I sometimes overwhelmed myself with the idea that I was misspending my days.

I told my father, "It's not always easy living in the shadow of your awareness of death." I didn't yet know how to design my life in accordance with his wisdom.

He told me that I would figure it out, but then rather callously fanned the flames of my angst. "I could never live like you and your brother: living in the same city—any city, for that matter—working in the same building and taking orders from a boss."

He was particularly hostile toward the idea of waiting until retirement to satisfy one's desires. Retirement planning was postponement, procrastination, a waste. And wasting time is a fate worse than death, in his eyes. No, that's not quite right: *It is death*. If my father was feeling cooped up during a New England winter, he'd ship his motorcycle to Southern California and ride it down the Baja peninsula with his motorcycle buddies.

Greg was 22 years old when he became self-employed as a general contractor. "I was on the porch with my father-in-law," he told me. "He was a talented carpenter and always talked about starting his own business, but he never did. I decided that night I was going to work for myself."

At the time, I was 2 years old, and Daniel was 6 months old. My father had $1,500 in the bank. He also didn't have a driver's license, so he rode a bicycle to his first job prospect. After he got the job, he told my mother: "Well, I got it, now I just need to figure out how to do it." He's been in business for thirty years, figuring it out every day, he says.

I felt as if I had spent several years ignoring the wisdom in my father's letters. Then I stumbled upon Oliver Sacks' essay "My Own Life" published in *The New York Times*. The neurologist and author had learned he had terminal cancer. I was moved by Sacks' humility and grace in the face of inevitable death.

My father and his mother talked about death often, but Sacks was actually dying. "It is up to me now to choose how to live out the months that remain to me," he wrote in his essay. "I have to live in the richest, deepest, most productive way I can."

After reading his autobiography *On the Move*, I decided to quit my job and embark on a walkabout, a time to reflect on my own life and eventual death. My pilgrimage would have three acts: First, I would backpack through China for three weeks. Second, I would spend six weeks in my hometown. Third, I would spend a month driving my 1982 Honda Nighthawk across the country to California.

As I was planning my travels, I wrote a letter to Sacks in which I thanked him for partly inspiring me to embark on an adventure of self-discovery. I wished him joy and peace in his final days and the satisfaction of knowing that he had lived a rich and productive life.

Several months later, I was in a hostel in Guilin, China, when I learned Sacks had passed away. It was at 3 a.m., but I was awake, my stomach in a revolt from food poisoning. I had spent an hour clutching my abdomen, groaning, and scrambling to and from the bathroom. I took an antibiotic and tried to distract myself with Facebook. As the pain began to fade, I saw the headline of Sacks' passing.

As I was leaving Kearsarge Cemetery, my phone buzzed in my pocket. My aunt Stephanie had called to help me narrow the search for Anne's gravestone to a small quadrant of the cemetery. I re-entered the graveyard with renewed confidence. It took fifteen minutes before I saw a decorative red hummingbird beside my grandmother's name on a gravestone. I had arrived. But I still didn't know why I had come. Perhaps I had visited the cemetery for the same reason my father wrote his letters—by acknowledging death, we make space for life.

I knelt at the gravestone and whispered an apology for not visiting more during high school. I followed with a thank you, for the safety and predictability she had provided when I was a boy ricocheting between parents after their split. It's rumored that Anne had nurtured my fondness for reading. I thanked her for that, too.

"A bird flew into a window at my father's house today," I said. "According to superstition, it means death is near."

Before I'd left to visit the cemetery, I looked up the old wives' tale online. I discovered that there was a more comforting interpretation. It also means change is near.

As I stood over the gravestone, I remembered the letter I had read aloud at Anne's funeral. My family huddled around me as I spoke, tears smacked the pages in my trembling hands. When I finished reading, my aunt told me that my grandmother had heard every word. If that were true, she could hear me now.

"Watch over me as I change, Nanny," I said. "Then you can rest your eyes forever."

CHAPTER 14

Hoedown at McDonald's

I tapped my foot to the sound of banjos as the McDonald's filled with Southerners. An elderly woman shuffled onto the floor to square dance. Others joined her, some clicking their tap shoes alone, others partnering off.

I was driving across the country on a 1982 Honda Nighthawk motorcycle and had checked into a hotel after a sixty-mile ride along the Blue Ridge Parkway in Virginia. I walked to the McDonald's next to my hotel looking for a quick meal.

When I entered, I thought I might've stumbled onto an American Legion meeting until I noticed musicians unpacking instruments at the back of the restaurant.

"Is there a performance tonight?" I asked the cashier.

"Bluegrass band," he yelled over the noise.

He said the Cranford Creek Bluegrass Band played for the local community at the McDonald's in Pilot Mountain, North Carolina, every Monday night. I'd planned on eating dinner in my room while watching the nightly news, but I couldn't miss a hoedown at Mickey D's.

The fast-food restaurant was packed with about fifty people wearing blue jeans, overalls, flannel shirts, and leather cut-off vests. They greeted friends at tables, shook hands, and exchanged stories. I heard a "hot diggity!" from the corner of the room.

A man in his forties wearing a handlebar mustache and a leather vest pulled a pair of white tap shoes from his bag and slid into the middle of the floor to improvise a tap number to "Your Cheatin' Heart" by Hank Williams.

When the song ended, the lead singer addressed the crowd through the microphone. "Just a reminder, y'all: This Saturday, we'll be at the country store—just playin' country."

The music paused, and the lead singer visited tables. Patricia, in her sixties, had short blonde hair and was wearing a white shirt, black pants, and dark Nikes with light green laces. With a southern drawl in her voice, she told me, "Every Monday, people come from all over, about a sixty-mile radius."

"Do you play?" I asked.

Patricia nodded, then balled up a fist. "I used to play banjo until the arthritis in my fingers got so bad I couldn't hold the instrument anymore."

She asked what had brought me to Pilot Mountain. I told her I was on a cross-country trip. I was hoping for a quiet night by myself, but I thought the community event was refreshing. Patricia could tell I had no intention of participating in the hoedown.

"How did you guys end up playing here?" I asked.

"Years ago, I asked the McDonald's manager if we could play for the community. I told him we wouldn't disturb customers or hold up any lines. He said, 'Don't worry about it. You play all ya want.'"

Patricia leaned in close and whispered, "There's another guy who plays in restaurants around here, but he's nothin' but a joke. Doesn't play well, and he eats enough for two people." She laughed, then said goodbye and visited other tables.

I walked in front of the band and snapped a picture with my phone. As I turned away, I heard the guitarist say, "That boy needs to learn how to flow."

I went back to my table and continued eating my dinner.

A woman in her sixties swung open the front door and shuffled into the restaurant with a cane. She said hello to friends and then visited my table.

"You married?" she asked.

I grinned with surprise and shook my head.

She lifted her cane. "Well, why not?"

"What do they put in sodas here?" I asked sarcastically.

She stretched out her hand, inviting me to dance.

"Maybe another time," I said, waving my hand.

She smiled as she shuffled off. "I'm gonna hold you to that."

When I returned to my hotel room, I thought about the guitarist's comment that I needed to learn how to flow. I wondered what exactly he meant by that. I think he meant I needed to learn how to participate—to join something, anything, to share values with a community, if only for a night.

I've always had trouble blending in with communities. At work, I resist wearing a company badge to signal that I'm part of the group, and I don't say "namaste" after a yoga session to feel in sync with the rest of class. But even a free spirit can value a community of folks who seem to dance as if no one is watching.

As I drifted off the sleep, I wondered if I would ever learn how to flow.

CHAPTER 15

Doubt Isn't Sexy

I didn't blow my chance with this woman because there wasn't chemistry. I didn't blow it over a lack of common interests. I blew it because I'm still figuring out my life, and women want men who have their life figured out, or at least appear to. Doubt says: "I'm not sure about me." Which can also say: "I'm not sure about you."

We met in a bar and strolled to a friend's hotel. She wrapped her arm around me, and I pulled her tight. She tripped on the escalator, but I caught her at the waist. Later, I applied a Band-Aid. Things progressed, became intimate. The next day she flew back to Austin, Texas, and put 2,000 miles between us. Texting. Weeks of banter. Then a day of nothing. A couple more days. Her name bumped down my phone's contact list.

On my motorcycle trip across the country, I visited her in Austin. I was just passing through on my way to a new job, new career, new life. We spent an afternoon taking in the city sights. Perched on a wall, feet dangling, we talked about relationships. Was she open to new beginnings? Maybe not, she wondered. Someone could sweep her off her feet, she admitted. Go ahead, I thought to myself. Sweep away.

But I was fumbling about, having ditched the steady office job to join the creatives on the Left Coast. I had traded answers for questions, salary for freelance, networks for solitude. The doubt those changes created had influenced my love life, producing a more vulnerable and less cool, confident version of me.

Later that night, we went out for pizza. I said that I was reading the work of William James, and her eyes wandered. I wasn't just doubtful; now I was boring. I used to be clever in conversation—quick with a quip or a pop culture reference.

As I was leaving a few hours later, she leaned against the mantle of the fireplace in her apartment. It was a moment to cross the room, perhaps give her a kiss. But I hesitated and missed the opportunity. An earlier version of myself would've crossed the room, but this version was doubtful and fainthearted. I knew if I tightened up my resume, applied to some communications jobs, and dropped this silly writing business, I'd return to my quick-witted, gutsier self.

The experience made me think that women want love interests with goals, but not ones who can't pay the utility bills. Having your life together matters during courtship. Maybe that means a law degree or middle management, or if you're one of those creative types, it could mean a book deal and published stuff. Something stable, secure. Women want winners, especially once they've reached their thirties. What do I have to offer besides hope that I'll find my way? You're working on a novel? That's cute.

That's all right, I thought to myself as I rode away. I wasn't lucky enough to find my calling in high school or college, even graduate school. I stumbled onto it in adulthood. Now I'm playing catch-up. But I'll be back in high places again. And maybe, if I see this woman again, I'll be sure about me, which means I'll be sure about her.

I don't know, though. I have my doubts.

CHAPTER 16

Keeping the Channel Open

When I first meet someone, I have a tendency to listen more than I talk. The habit has granted me access to unique stories and perspectives, but it occasionally leads to a form of conversation misconduct, where I become prisoner to a string of monologues that leave me feeling exploited, chewed up, and spit out.

I was reading in a coffee shop in Long Beach, California, when I heard someone behind me ask, "What book are you reading?"

I turned to see an elderly man sitting in a chair with a laptop perched on his knees.

"*Adventures in the Screen Trade*," I said. "It's a book about the film industry and screenwriting written by the famous screenwriter, William Goldman."

I could barely finish my sentence before the man told me everything he knew about the movie business, Los Angeles, and the "art" of storytelling.

"Ah, they're all weirdoes in Hollywood. It's all about the money, you know. Have you seen *Bridges Over Madison County*? Now *that's* a movie. Meryl Streep was perfect, the other guy was terrible."

I listened and nodded, realizing the man had little interest in having a conversation. By "conversation," I mean, "An informal exchange of ideas by spoken words," as the word is defined. Keyword: "exchange." For me, a good conversation is like a tennis match. You talk, I talk, back and forth we go.

When I visited Paris, I observed people in coffee shops leaning forward in their seats as they spoke, their eyes locked, bodies erect. The interactions had electricity to them. Everyone was engaged. The exchanges seemed balanced. They were tennis matches. Perhaps it's no surprise that conversation was elevated to an art form in French salons. Such conversations recall another definition of conversation: "social intercourse."

It wasn't my hope to engage in social intercourse with this man. It was just small talk, after all. But I would have settled for a friendly tennis match. I considered politely saying, "It was nice speaking with you, but—"

Instead, I kept listening.

"I used to visit the homes of celebrities," the man continued. "I sold cell phones before people knew about cell phones, when the only people who bought them were celebrities and crooks."

I responded with more head-nodding, more "mm, hmm'ing." I began to feel like the character Neal Page played by Steve Martin in the movie *Planes, Trains and Automobiles*. After spending several days with an obnoxious travel companion—Dell Griffith, played by John Candy—Neal says that Dell reminds him of a talking doll that pulls its own string.

"Didn't you notice on the plane when you started talking, eventually, I started reading the vomit bag?" Neal says in a tirade. "Didn't that give you some sort of clue that, hey, maybe this guy isn't enjoying it? You know: Everything is not an antidote; you have to discriminate. You choose things that are funny or mildly amusing or interesting. You're a miracle. Your stories have none of that. They're not even amusing, accidentally. And, by the way, when you're telling one of your little stories, here's a good idea: Have a point! It makes it so much more interesting for the listener!"

In the coffee shop, the man asked me why I had moved to California, then reacted to my answer with a tangent, then steered the conversation toward the artwork in his Etsy account. Then we were "discussing" his work schedule. Then we were browsing his website. Then I was holding his business card.

When I couldn't stomach another monologue, I closed my book. "Well, it was nice talking to you, but I should get going." As I was leaving, I felt sorry for future victims who might fall into this man's web of personal anecdotes.

The next day, he emailed me with an idea for a story. Before I responded, I re-watched *Planes, Trains and Automobiles*. I paid special attention to the hotel scene where Neal erupts in anger over Dell's behavior. Had I become like Steve Martin's character? Cynical, intolerant, someone who explains the rules of conversation to "abusers"?

A few days later, I stumbled upon another definition for the phrase *small talk*: "Keeping the channel open." On the surface, a conversation may seem to be about the weather or books or movies, but it's really about establishing a connection, a means of recognizing our shared humanity.

That day in the coffee shop, I crossed paths with someone who talks more than he listens. But that doesn't mean he's a meandering kook or a selfish loudmouth. He just wanted to open a channel. And I'm glad he did.

CHAPTER 17

Fake It 'til You Make It

For most of my twenties, I was a magical thinker. During this period of my life, I was reading a lot of self-help books, including the best-selling *The Secret*, and though I was in a Ph.D. program to study physiology for five years, *The Secret* had me believing I could do anything, have anything, *be* anything; all I had to do was ask the universe.

If becoming financially free was only a matter of making requests of the cosmos' abundant piggy bank and holding my desires in my mind, why wouldn't I ask to become a millionaire by 30? Why stop there? Why couldn't I write a commercial novel that would shoot to the top of bestsellers lists with the velocity of a Dan Brown thriller?

The spell began to break when my thirtieth birthday came and went and my wishes hadn't been fulfilled: I wasn't rich. My novel hadn't attracted an agent; instead, I self-published. And like most of my friends, my talents were being exploited for profit in Corporate America. What had happened? How had I been so easily duped by *The Secret*'s tantalizing messages?

I later realized I was predisposed to the state of mind self-help books exploit.

When I was younger, my parents—especially my father—had a cliché for everything. For struggle, he claimed, "Where there's a will, there's a way;" for pain, "What doesn't kill you makes you stronger;" for trauma, "Let the past be the past." On birthdays, he'd announce half-kiddingly, "Today is the first day of the rest of your life." His adages helped inform him, instruct him, and inspire him.

They did the same for me in adolescence and into early adulthood. Like my parents, I had a motto or cliché ready for most situations. For work: "A rolling stone gathers no moss." For hardship: "Don't worry; be happy." For imposter syndrome: "Fake it 'til you make it." To pay homage to my father, I collected his favorite axioms into a book, *Life According to Dad*, and gave it to him for Father's Day.

Using clichés to guide my life worked until my late twenties, when they began to lose their potency. After graduating with a master's degree, I became a marketing writer for businesses and nonprofits in Boston. I lived in the city, working on complex problems with smart people from diverse backgrounds, most of whom didn't view the world through rose-colored glasses.

I've been an idea person throughout my career. Many of my ideas, which can often be categorized as "big picture," have been implemented in anything from advertising campaigns and event themes to product names and product messaging. But whenever I used clichés to propose a solid idea in the workplace, others took me less seriously. Without acknowledging potential unintended consequences, I might come off as unrealistic, impractical, or too rosy.

I once helped build and drive the vision for a company's blog, but I underestimated the time and technical resources needed to develop and maintain it. At lunch, I reflected on the process and dropped a quote from Napoleon Hill's *Think and Grow Rich*: "Whatever the mind of man can conceive and believe, it can achieve." My coworkers thought I was naive, perhaps even delusional.

Clichés had helped structure my way of thinking, but they had become inadequate. They didn't reflect the complex environments and circumstances of my adulthood. After a period of disillusionment, I knew I had to change. I started questioning the clichés and the way I dealt with reality.

Clichés, I realized, were too biased toward the positive at the expense of potential dark possibilities. When "times get tough," it's not always easy for the "tough" to "get going." Sometimes, we're just flat-out beat, and it's wise to retreat, regroup, and reflect so we can "fight another day." I was always told to "keep my head up," but sometimes it's tough not to lower it in defeat. While "smooth seas never made for skillful sailors," storms hurt and can even break us.

Clichés no longer rang true for me because life wasn't always easy or sunny. Reality didn't always bend to my will. I pursued my goals, but they were tougher to achieve than I expected. I took wrong turns. Systems were unfair; folks were unkind. People let me down, insulted me, betrayed me.

In my late twenties and early thirties, I started accepting that life is as much disaster as triumph. We don't always get into the school or program we seek. The job or career we want might not want us. Love can go unrequited. Financial setbacks happen. Accidents occur. Illness can strike. People lie. People die. By encouraging us to always stay positive, the clichés deny the reality we must face.

I eventually found a way to deliver my first death blow to the clichés that ran my life: therapy. My therapist was a social worker and a psychoanalytically-informed therapist not much older than me, so we were dealing with similar life-stage problems. His approach didn't involve dispensing advice as a life coach might. Rather, he encouraged his patients to evaluate their reality objectively. To see themselves clearly. When people thought critically about themselves and their circumstances, they didn't need advice, he reasoned, because they would know what to do.

Following his guidance, I realized my parents had raised me in a rather uncritical environment. Their philosophy was to "let sleeping dogs lie." We avoided reflecting on pesky matters like what made us sad or mad lest we make things worse and cause new problems. For instance, if I had asked my parents about their divorce, they wouldn't understand why I couldn't leave well enough alone.

Such an uncritical environment ensures that nobody ever thinks about anything. And if someone doesn't know what they think about something, they don't know how they feel about it either. Using clichés is a way to avoid thinking. "Leave the past in the past" was the perfect countermeasure to talking about the trauma of my parents' divorce. Clichés robbed us of the chance to acknowledge it. They robbed us of the chance to heal so the pain wouldn't resurface in inexplicable ways, like overwork or substance abuse.

Despite the importance of thinking, therapy taught me that thinking is difficult, another reason some might want to avoid it. It takes time and energy to think through complicated matters, and people are always having to expand their vocabulary for puzzling issues.

Thinking is also messy. A person seldom comes to a complete understanding of the issues they face. Before therapy, whenever I might have reached the edge of my understanding, I'd employ a cliché that approximated my thoughts or feelings on the matter. But in therapy, I checked my clichés at the door. I was pushed to find words for how I thought or felt about events or people that troubled me. I rambled and talked nonsense, but insights came. Sometimes, we would unlock something that had been a mystery.

Living and working in rural New Hampshire, where my parents have spent their entire adult lives, is simpler. One can often get away with using clichés to navigate and interpret life in such rural settings. In the city, however, where I've worked in modern offices, life isn't black-and-white but shades of gray. Negotiating city and corporate life requires more complex systems of thought. While rural life might lead to simplistic thinking, city life can lead folks to become critical and cynical.

I wanted to evolve past my uncritical origins, but I didn't want to go too far in the other direction and become a coldhearted cynic or nihilist. I still wanted to believe I had some control over my life. I just needed to find values, systems, and worldviews that accepted that life was sometimes unfair, often indifferent to our wishes, and actively resistant to our desires.

Enter the second death blow to living a clichéd life: philosophy or the love of wisdom. In my thirties, I replaced new-age and self-help guides with philosophy. I read books on Eastern philosophy, like Lao Tzu's *Tao Te Ching* and Confucius's *Analects*, and on Western philosophy, like Plato's *Republic* and Marcus Aurelius' *Meditations*. I joined philosophy groups, watched documentaries, and read biographies on Friedrich Nietzsche, Viktor Frankl, and Jean-Paul Sartre, among others.

Stoic philosophy was undergoing a resurgence at the time, and the tradition helped me cope with day-to-day challenges. For example, stoics believe that events don't harm people as much as their judgments of the events do. Marcus Aurelius, a Roman emperor, encourages readers not to worry about things outside their control; instead, they should act on things within their control. Stoics also recommend living in accordance with one's nature. If someone is athletic, they should do athletic things. If they're brainy, they should do intellectual things. Such philosophy equipped me for life while also allowing me to accept its complexities.

Philosophy also helped me manage the dread that started to creep in as I approached midlife: knowing I was going to die one day. Enter existentialism.

The philosophical tradition of existentialism has been described as less a school of thought and more a mood or attitude toward life. It deals with matters such as anxiety, death, authenticity, isolation, and the search for meaning in one's existence. More than any other philosophical tradition, existentialism has helped me address the realization that life lacks intrinsic meaning.

"No why. Just here," as the composer and philosopher, John Cage, put it when *Life* magazine asked him about the meaning of life.

Faced with this understanding, I had to invent meaning for my life to avoid despair. But how? Jean-Paul Sartre's idea that humans are radically free was both terrifying and exhilarating. According to him, "existence precedes essence." In other words, no one is born with innate character traits. Rather, we construct who we are with every choice we make.

Albert Camus also agreed that life has no intrinsic meaning and reasoned it was absurd to seek meaning from a universe indifferent to our desires. He urges us to rebel against life's absurdity by finding meaning in our relationships, our families, and our projects. In his famous essay *The Myth of Sisyphus*, Camus compares life's absurdity to the punishment of Sisyphus, a figure in Greek mythology who was condemned to spend eternity rolling a boulder up a mountain, only for it to roll back down whenever he neared the summit. While Sisyphus was punished to forever perform a meaningless activity, Camus suggests that perhaps Sisyphus could find some joy in the absurdity of rolling the boulder. Maybe Sisyphus could even learn to be happy in his fate.

Once I accepted that the only meaning my life would have was the meaning I gave it, I began to engage in meaningful activities I found enjoyable, like writing: the final death blow to living a clichéd life.

Back when I started writing in my late twenties, I fell into every possible cliché trap. Let's say I was writing a fictional action sequence where the hero confronts the villain, his former mentor, in a dramatic climax. In their final duel, the hero might get off a perfect shot, fatally wounding the villain.

"Great shot," the villain might say, holding a hand over his bleeding stomach.

In that moment, the hero would likely say something like, "I learned from the best."

Alas, I couldn't keep that. It's a cliché! And they are off-limits for writers. Why? A cliché might once have conveyed a truth, but readers have encountered it so often in movies and books, it no longer has the impact it used to. Through study and practice, I've learned that all good writing is a never-ending war on clichés. A writer must always search for fresh language. If I accidentally employ a cliché—which happens often—I strike it out in revision. This practice of avoiding clichés on the page has found its way into my life.

When I reflect on my evolution from a magical to a critical thinker, I realize that using clichés for so long allowed me to rely on the wisdom of others while I figured out who I was and what I thought. They gave me something to hold on to during the painstaking process of updating how I viewed and thought about myself and the world.

Now, in my late thirties, I realize the cost of not relying on clichés. They allowed me to avoid the difficult task of thinking. They allowed me to deny reality, which can be difficult to see clearly. Ignorance was bliss. Without clichés, life is messier, more nuanced, and sometimes incomprehensible. But "the truth hurts," right?

PART III

Found

2018–2023

You must be ready to burn yourself in your own flame; how could you rise anew if you have not first become ashes?

—Friedrich Nietzsche

CHAPTER 18

The Gift of Pain

I was in Pasadena, California, looking after a cat for a friend of mine. What I had initially embraced as a writing retreat quickly became a nightmare. I was trying to write at a desk in the living room when my back went into spasm, causing me worrying pain. Trying to distract myself, I opened Netflix and watched a new documentary about the history of cancer.

Until then, I'd thought the several months of off-and-on back pain was the result of an injury—a musculoskeletal issue from running or riding a motorcycle, perhaps—but my anxiety over the pain's chronicity had been growing. Partway through the documentary, the angst reached a fever pitch. Fueled, no doubt, by the film's subject matter, I became convinced that I had a tumor in my spine. I was sure of it. I now had cancer. The idea filled me with dread. My mind raced with possibilities, and I began hyperventilating. I was having a panic attack.

It had been nearly a year since I moved to Southern California to explore screenwriting after I quit my science writing job in Cambridge, Massachusetts. In that time, I had gone from a high-functioning working professional to a hypochondriac—obsessed with every ache and pain and overwhelmed by the fear of illness. As a freelance writer in California, I didn't have a steady income, and obtaining health insurance was a nightmare. Every day, questions about the most basic things spiraled through my head: Will I run out of money? Will my insurance cover that X-ray of my lower back? Am I going crazy? Bouts of grinding back pain evolved into free-floating angst. I was chronically on edge and reacted strongly to perceived threats. My nervous system felt stuck in the "on" position.

Unsurprisingly, I was finding it difficult to break into screenwriting, and the way I had gone about trying to do so was romantic and unrealistic. The first screenplay I wrote had won second place in a contest and received favorable reviews from a couple of members of the industry. But I was halfway through my second screenplay when I arrived in California and couldn't push away an existential angst that I was doomed to fail. I felt the impossibility—the futility—of building a career in the movie business. I got the impression that I could write for ten years and never get anywhere.

Curiously, I had moved to California to write for the screen, and all I ended up writing was essays and journalism. What was I doing? I should have been in Boston writing for businesses and working on a novel. Instead, I had quit my job at a prestigious biomedical research institute in Cambridge, where I'd written for biomedical scientists from MIT and Harvard. I was untethered from the workforce, making trips to social services to secure health insurance and using food stamps to buy food. I was "following my dreams," to be sure, but it had left me poor and dependent. Having always prided myself on self-reliance, I was disturbed by such vulnerability. I wasn't in complete control anymore. Things were uncertain. I had always striven to be a somebody; now I was a nobody.

Months before Pasadena, I had visited my primary care physician in Long Beach, California, thinking I had strained a muscle in my back during a hard run on a treadmill. I called to check on the results of an X-ray of my spine. The 80-year-old physician read me the radiology report over the phone.

"It says you have an L5 retrolisthesis."

"What does that mean?" I asked, concerned.

"The report says your lowest lumbar vertebra, L5, has slipped backward five millimeters."

More worried, I asked, "What does *that* mean?"

"I don't know exactly, but I'll refer you to a back specialist."

"What should I do in the meantime?"

"Maybe try a back brace?"

Wait a minute, I thought. I'm 33 years old, with no history of mental or physical problems, a life-long athlete, and now I need a back brace? As many of us often do, I turned to the Internet. I read about "retrolisthesis" and obsessed over my radiology report. After reading about disc degeneration, ruptured and herniated discs, misalignments of vertebra, fractures, arthritis, spinal cord tears, and spinal instability, I began to invent worst-case scenarios. As I descended into neurosis, my body—slowly, incrementally—began to go haywire.

Sometimes, I woke up at night and my right arm would be alarmingly numb, taking several minutes to wake up. My right hand constantly ached after I had been working on my laptop. I experienced numbness in the fingers of my right hand after pressing them against a hard surface. Tingling radiated down the back of my legs and into my calves, which I referred to as "zings" or "fireworks." I was chronically constipated and had reoccurring hemorrhoids and anal fissures that produced blood in my stool. I was seeing dark specks in my eyes that an optometrist called "floaters." The glands in my neck were chronically swollen, and I was prone to reoccurring sore throats. There was a worrying ache in my right testicle. My joints cracked, popped, and ached. Some nights, I would wake up gasping. The next day, I would be bone-crushingly fatigued.

Weeks after Pasadena, I requested an MRI on my lower back, only to discover that I had tears near a spinal nerve root and degeneration of my L5 vertebra. I met with the back specialist again in a worried state.

"Tears? Degeneration?" I said with dread. "I hope I don't need surgery. I don't want to go down the opioid route."

"There's nothing seriously wrong with your back," the orthopedist explained in a calm tone. "Those abnormalities aren't likely causing your pain. You have an average amount of disc degeneration and arthritis for your age. It's a natural part of aging."

He was telling me that I was healthy. I had never felt more ill.

I became a medical-device company's dream; I bought every conceivable ergonomic solution: a laptop riser, an exercise ball for sitting, and an anti-fatigue mat for standing. Nothing helped.

The next bouts of back pain lasted longer.

At that point, I ruminated that I might have a serious condition. I became intensely fearful, a bona fide hypochondriac. I muted pharmaceutical commercials about rheumatoid arthritis or fibromyalgia because I thought I might have the conditions and felt woozy as actors dramatized them for the public. If you mentioned the word cancer, my skin crawled. I had to stop a friend mid-conversation as he told me about his father's cancer diagnosis.

Every time I met with my primary care doctor to discuss the reoccurring pain in my back, I left feeling more stressed. If he couldn't provide some explanation for my symptoms, my imagination would invent any number of improbable disorders. The reflective thinking that sustained my writing career had turned on me. It probably didn't help that I was watching a lot of news and was troubled by the social and political uncertainty around Donald Trump's run for president. In my leisure time, I watched the television series *House*. I was also reading a memoir called *Brain on Fire*, written by a reporter named Susannah Cahalan. She had spent a harrowing month struggling with a devastating and mysterious illness known as "anti-NMDA receptor encephalitis," a rare autoimmune disease that can attack the brain.

After months of visiting many doctors, from physical therapists to psychologists, rheumatologists to neurologists, and exploring physical therapy and ergonomics, I began to wonder whether I was experiencing a condition that was less a problem of the body and more a problem of the mind. I read and read, eventually discovering the work of a New York physician named John Sarno, MD, who passed away in 2017. Dr. Sarno pioneered the diagnosis of a condition called tension myoneural syndrome, or TMS—a psychosomatic syndrome in which repressed, unconscious emotions, most often anger, manifest as physical symptoms to distract the conscious mind from painful emotions.

Though it wasn't widely accepted among the medical community, Dr. Sarno stood by his theory that most chronic pain conditions, including back or neck pain, fibromyalgia or carpal tunnel syndrome, and even some autoimmune disorders, aren't physical problems but psychological ones, all under the umbrella of TMS. He speculated that evolution had built into our brains tools to avoid dealing with stress below the level of conscious awareness. Developing physical symptoms, according to Dr. Sarno, served to distract us from unpleasant emotions. In Dr. Sarno's rehabilitation practice, if a patient accepted that their pain had psychological roots, they would typically recover, even after years of doctor visits and countless interventions.

In his decades-long career treating patients with chronic back pain, Dr. Sarno found that individuals who developed TMS had similar personality characteristics. In his book *The Mindbody Prescription*, he wrote,

"Deeply repressed feelings of inadequacy foster the development of personality traits that are almost universal to people with TMS. They tend to be perfectionistic, compulsive, highly conscientious, and ambitious; they are driven, self-critical, and generally successful. They also have a compulsion to please, be a good person, to be helpful and non-confrontational. In short, people with TMS have a strong need for approval, whether it is love, admiration, or respect." He writes that self-imposed pressures to please, to be a "good" person, and to achieve cause inner conflict. The lingering child within each of us doesn't want to be put under pressure. If it's pushed, it can get sad and angry and cause pain.

Among those who have suffered from chronic back pain, Dr. Sarno is a cult figure, with a 90 percent success rate in curing chronic pain patients. In *The Mindbody Prescription*, he claims that, since 1973, he has seen about ten thousand patients who have been rendered pain-free. In 1999, John Stossel, then a journalist for ABC, hosted a 20/20 segment about Dr. Sarno's work and his own back pain. High-profile figures who report being cured by Dr. Sarno's work include radio talk show host Howard Stern and the creator of *Seinfeld*, Larry David. A filmmaker who has suffered from TMS his whole life recently made a documentary, *All the Rage*, which profiles Dr. Sarno and includes an interview with Larry David. David says that realizing his chronic arm pain was psychological, and not tendinitis, "was the closest thing I've ever had to a religious experience. And I wept."

On Amazon.com, Dr. Sarno's books have received thousands of reviews featuring stories of transformation. Many of these people had seen numerous doctors without success but say they were cured within weeks of reading his books, especially the best-selling book *Healing Back Pain*. Integrative physician Dr. Andrew Weil wrote in his book *Spontaneous Healing* that Dr. Sarno's impressive record of clinical success was based on nothing more than talking to patients and enlightening them as to the true nature of their pain. Dr. Weil called Dr. Sarno equal parts doctor, scientist, and faith healer.

When Dr. Sarno began his career in rehabilitative medicine at New York State Rehabilitation Hospital over fifty years ago, many of his patients suffered from various pain syndromes and had received conventional treatments, such as physical therapy, without fully recovering. Most of his patients became stuck in cycles of pain management, which required regular office visits and endless treatments. Dr. Sarno became frustrated. He wasn't addressing the root causes of his patients' chronic pain. He became puzzled by the fact that chronic back pain was becoming an epidemic, growing at a rate of fourteen times that of population growth at that time.

He noticed that nearly all of his patients with chronic back pain had similar medical histories. In addition to their back pain, many suffered from conditions that were caused by psychological stress. Many suffered from chronic migraines, respiratory issues, such as asthma, or pet allergies. Others had irritable bowel syndrome or skin diseases like eczema. Were pain conditions, such as chronic lower back pain, caused by stress and tension, or even emotional problems?

With this understanding in mind, Dr. Sarno began informing his patients that their back pain might be caused by unconscious stress. After ruling out serious conditions like cancer, he would explain to his patients that their physical symptoms were trying to distract them from unpleasant emotions. Many of the patients who accepted that their back pain was largely psychological experienced a full recovery, even after years of doctor visits and countless interventions.

In *Healing Back Pain*, Dr. Sarno explains that, in most cases, pain wasn't a structural issue, such as a herniated disc or disc degeneration. More than likely, it was caused by mild oxygen deprivation, brought about by the brain altering the blood flow to an area. If a person was ignoring unconscious anger, for example, their mind might distract them from the anger by depriving their lower back of oxygen. Tension myoneural syndrome isn't recognized by mainstream medicine, yet tens of thousands of people have cured themselves of chronic pain just by acknowledging that their pain isn't an anatomical or physiological problem but a psychosomatic one.

The cure for TMS is knowledge. It consists simply of reading Dr. Sarno's books or, when he was alive, attending his Monday-night lectures or making an appointment with him. Exposing oneself to this knowledge would help reveal to the conscious mind the repressed negative emotions, such as sadness or anger, that was driving the pain. In Dr. Weil's book *Natural Health, Natural Medicine*, he writes that "most people with chronic back pain go around thinking they have a bad back and that the trouble is there. In my experience, all chronic back (and neck) pain should be considered TMS until proven otherwise, and most therapeutic effort should be directed at your head: specifically, at changing your patterns of thinking, feeling, and handling stress that lead the nervous system into this abnormal pattern."

Dr. Weil once experienced an episode of disabling back pain. After he accepted the emotional basis for the pain—the loss of two close relationships—his back pain disappeared in three weeks and never returned. After that, he recommended Dr. Sarno's books to patients who had already tried every imaginable treatment for back pain.

Of course, I didn't accept the diagnosis of TMS right away. Believing I was developing a serious physiological disorder, I continued to see countless doctors and underwent a number of procedures. I told doctors about my worsening back pain, reoccurring hemorrhoids, anal fissures, muscle aches, fatigue, and tingling and numbness in my limbs.

When tests ruled out autoimmune and neurological diseases, including rheumatoid arthritis, Lyme disease, STDs, and cancer, I ruminated on obscure infections, particularly as related to my three-week backpacking trip in China, where I had gone before I moved to California. I had gotten sick after eating a chicken noodle dish. I had had stomach pain, diarrhea, and a fever. The illness had lasted a day, and I never saw a doctor.

Most doctors dismissed the possibility of an infection with troubling quickness. And yet, I told them, I had never experienced any major mental or physical health problems until after that travel experience. What about reactive arthritis, joint pain, and swelling triggered by an infection in another part of the body, I suggested? Reactive arthritis often results from an infection tied to bacteria that enters the gastrointestinal tract from contaminated food. Most people fully recover, but it may take a few months to a year. Some people have long-term symptoms.

No doctor could give me a definitive answer.

The first panic attack landed me in an emergency room in Long Beach, desperate and confused. At home an hour before, I had begun fixating on my aching testicle and breathing shallowly. Pacing the kitchen, I coughed and dry-heaved and then began to hyperventilate and panic over the possibilities. At the ER, a nurse gave me a lorazepam, and a social worker gave me a list of psychiatrists in the area. A week later, when I told my story to a psychiatrist, he leaned back in his chair and said, "You're like a bear that left its cave and got its butt kicked. Maybe you should move back to Boston to lick your wounds?" It took me two months to come to terms with his advice, but he was right. My California dream was dead.

When I returned to Boston, a friend of my father's noticed the timidity in my demeanor and fear in my eyes. A subscriber to alternative medicine, she offered her thoughts. "I know you have a practical, scientific approach to medicine, but my feeling is that your problems are a physical manifestation of an emotional state. Your energy feels stuck."

She recommended I try a therapy called Tapping, an emotional release technique that involved recalling traumatic events from my past while using two fingers to physically tap areas of my face that correlated with meridian points. The technique was supposed to facilitate the release of suppressed emotions. The technique's potency seemed to be less about the tapping of the meridian points on the face and chest and more about the naming and voicing aloud of troubling emotions.

During my first Tapping session, I cried harder than I'd ever cried in my life. I noticed an emotional charge surrounding my failed relationship with my ex-girlfriend Paige, which I realized I hadn't grieved. After my first session, I flipped through a photo album and dwelled on happy moments of that relationship. I wept more. Afterward, I felt that something had been dislodged.

I landed a job as a writer in the marketing department at a major hospital in Boston. Under pressure to write several articles in a short period of time, I came down with viral pharyngitis in my first week.

Days later, an anal fissure reopened. For the next three weeks, every bowel movement produced a sharp cutting sensation in my rectum. My mind fixated on the pain. Any healing that happened while I slept was undone each morning. Each night, I went to bed dreading the next morning. I couldn't sit, walk, or drive without searing pain in my rectum. Sitting on a donut pillow provided little relief. I desperately hoped the fissure wouldn't require surgical repair.

A gastroenterologist prescribed a rectal cream, which I applied three times a day for a month. Thankfully, the fissure healed.

Once the fissure was healed, the gastroenterologist wanted to perform a sigmoidoscopy, a procedure that lets the doctor look inside the first part of the colon using a flexible tube. As a precaution, I asked him to perform a full colonoscopy instead. After the procedure, the gastroenterologist entered my room and closed the curtain.

"Your colon's perfectly clean, no polyps. I found an internal hemorrhoid, but it was too small to remove."

I got the sense that I shouldn't have been there. At 33 years old, I was too young for a colonoscopy. The doctor looked at me with sympathy and tilted his head.

"I saw from your chart that you've been dealing with anxiety."

"Wouldn't anyone be anxious with my symptoms?" I asked.

It was the first time a doctor had confronted me with the possibility that my symptoms had a psychological origin. However, I wasn't ready to accept a psychosomatic diagnosis. I still thought I might have a serious condition in the making. I shook my head in disappointment. Another test, another dead end.

A hypochondriac writing for a hospital was not a good mix. Every day, I read and wrote about diseases while my mind continued to roam for a diagnosis of my own. Like a first-year medical student, I thought I had every condition imaginable.

After a visit with my new primary care doctor, I was granted access to my blood work. Since I didn't know how to interpret the data, I would see an elevated number and be filled with dread. After scouring the Internet, I could make a rock-solid case for some intractable disease. Some of my symptoms did suggest rheumatoid arthritis (I had aching and cracking joints and an elevated rheumatoid factor). Ankylosing spondylitis didn't seem to be too far a stretch, either. With each discovered possibility, I would email my doctor an overly detailed and fearful message.

At one point, an immunologist found a previous Epstein-Barr virus (EBV) infection, which had caused mononucleosis when I was eighteen. Perhaps running myself ragged at the keyboard had triggered chronic mononucleosis? I eagerly brought up this possible infection hypothesis with several specialists. Had the infection caused reactive arthritis? Perhaps I had contracted trichinosis from undercooked meat? Giardiasis? Hep A? Polio?

Avian flu? Had China's food changed the colonies of bacteria in my gut, triggering an autoimmune reaction? What about Guillain-Barre syndrome, a rare neurological disorder that can follow a viral infection?

Not likely, responded my doctors, and I was sent on my way.

A few weeks later, after a wedding weekend in Washington, DC, I experienced my most severe bout of back pain. It was debilitating, and I barely slept for two weeks, as every sleeping position caused pain, even when I slept with a heating pad or an ice pack. At my work desk, I was constantly in pain, occasionally breaking into tears in my office. Undermined by the pain, I lost energy, focus, and drive, or "the will to thrive," as it's said in medicine.

For a month, all I thought about was the pain. I would get home from work and put ice on my back for hours. I couldn't exercise or socialize. I was a shadow of myself, convinced I was disabled. I had reached a place of helplessness, essentially giving in after repeated failed attempts to get better. I had tried a wedge cushion to elevate my knees as I put ice on my back. I'd tried an inversion table, a strap system to promote proper posture in my work chair, a new recliner, a new mattress, a lumbar roll, a foam roller, a back brace, every type of pain-relieving cream on the market, a heating pad, and stretches for the psoas muscle and iliotibial band. After countless unsuccessful treatments, I thought nothing would help.

My primary care physician was troubled by my responses to the depression questionnaire and prescribed an antidepressant.

The hypochondria intensified after my aunt, a nurse practitioner, suggested that, with my symptoms, I was likely in the throes of a developing autoimmune disorder of which our family had a history. She had psoriatic arthritis, and my maternal aunt had rheumatoid arthritis. My aunt suggested that my back pain might be ankylosing spondylitis, a degenerative and incurable autoimmune condition that affects the backs of men my age.

This sent my hypochondria into dark places. I immediately met with a rheumatologist, who ruled out the condition as fast as it took me to brief him on my state of health. Increasingly worried and desperate for answers, I visited the emergency room, complaining of back and neck pain, as well as joint pain. ER doctors could only offer ways to manage the pain. They wrote me prescriptions for lidocaine patches and naproxen cream and encouraged me to stick with physical therapy.

On my third visit to the ER, I got the sense that my medical chart was haunting me—undermining me—everywhere I went. I think the doctors looked at my chart, noted anxiety, and concluded that my troubles were psychological, not physical. They could then absolve themselves of responsibility and seemed to feel no guilt in discharging a patient in obvious distress.

To be fair, I wasn't exactly a patient a doctor would want to help; I was neurotic. They also probably thought my visits were serving an emotional purpose, known in medicine as a "secondary gain"—an unconscious desire on the part of the sufferer to benefit from support, sympathy, or prescriptions.

I tried to help diagnose myself in visits with my doctors. I didn't feel this was out of line, considering I'm a science writer with a master's in physiology. In some cases, I think the doctors pitied me because I misinterpreted my symptoms and was clearly illness-obsessed.

I once told my primary care physician, who was especially annoyed with me, that my body seemed to *need* something to hurt. I suggested fibromyalgia, a disorder in which patients complain of "hurting all over." It seemed to fit, as the pain migrated around my body: from my back to my neck, a hand to an Achilles tendon, or even a testicle. He dismissed fibromyalgia, saying it was a "diagnosis of exclusion." From his perspective, my problem was anxiety. He needed me to understand that I was healthy. He urged me to see clearly. The subtext of our meetings was that psychiatry was my only hope.

It wasn't until I was sitting in a waiting room before a psychotherapy session that I finally began to think my problems might, indeed, be psychosomatic, despite experiencing many physical symptoms. On a table in the waiting room was a copy of Psychology Today. One particular article caught my eye: "When the Body Speaks" by neurologist Suzanne O'Sullivan, MD. It was about psychosomatic illness. "Almost any symptoms we can imagine can become real when we are in distress—tremor, fatigue, speech impairments, numbness. Anything."

After that, I bought a copy of Dr. O'Sullivan's book *Is It All in Your Head? True Stories of Imaginary Illness*. In this fascinating book, she says, "There is no single solution to psychosomatic illness. To look for one is akin to looking for the cure for unhappiness. There is no single answer because there is no single cause. Sometimes you just have to figure out what purpose the illness serves, find what is missing and try to replace it. If the illness seems to be helping solve the problem of loneliness, then treat the loneliness and the illness will disappear. Or if the problem lies in the maladaptive response to messages the body sends, that can be relearned: break the patterns of fear and avoidance. Or if there's a specific trauma triggering the illness, then address it."

I began to examine my long list of recent life changes through the lens of psychosomatic illness. My decision to quit my job the year prior, backpack through China for three weeks, and then drive my motorcycle across the country to support myself on creative nonfiction in an unfamiliar state, in a housing situation that had become dysfunctional, without the support system of family or friends, had destroyed my normal routines, resulted in isolation, and caused tremendous unconscious stress.

As the physiatrist and trauma researcher Bessel A. van der Kolk, MD, wrote in *The Body Keeps the Score*, "Most people cannot tolerate being disengaged from others for any amount of time. People who cannot connect through work, friendships, or family usually find other ways of bonding, usually through illnesses, lawsuits, or family feuds. Anything is preferable to that Godforsaken sense of irrelevance or alienation."

Had my mind created an illness as a way for me to deal with all my life changes?

As months passed in Boston, I followed breadcrumbs through the field of psychosomatic medicine, reading all of Sarno's work. The diagnosis of TMS made sense to me. Even if the theory was nonsense, it at least had a placebo effect. It helped convince me that my body wasn't physically damaged, as my X-ray or MRI findings might have suggested.

I tried to loosen my grip on a structural explanation for my back pain. I considered the possibility that I didn't have a "bad back." If the muscles in my back felt tense or spasmed, I attempted to consciously relax them. I took Epsom salt baths to reduce muscle tension. I began swimming and doing yoga several times a week. Whenever I felt my back or shoulders tense, I tried to "breathe into them" or go for a walk. I stopped using ice on my back, stopped using lidocaine patches, and stopped taking the naproxen and Tylenol. Even if I was in pain, I tried to arrange dinners and drinks with friends or family. Understanding that I wasn't "broken" encouraged me to further engage with dynamic exercises and resume normal, everyday activities.

Around this time, I found a fascinating clue in one of my favorite books, *Travels*, a memoir by Michael Crichton, author of best sellers *Jurassic Park* and *The Andromeda Strain*. In Crichton's last year at Harvard Medical School, where he had been writing paperback thrillers to pay for med school, he made the decision to continue writing fiction over pursuing a career in medicine. In *Travels*, Crichton wrote that the choice had weighed heavily on him. He developed a paralyzing weakness in his right arm. He was convinced it was multiple sclerosis, but doctors could find nothing physically wrong with him. A neurologist suggested hysteria, or conversion disorder, a condition where emotional troubles are expressed as, or "converted into," physical symptoms. With no other explanation, Crichton finally accepted that his symptoms were a "somatization of psychological stress." He went on with his life. Six months later, the weakness vanished just as mysteriously as it had appeared.

It sounded an awful lot like TMS.

With Crichton's story in mind, I examined the previous life changes that might have been causing my emotional problems, and thus physical symptoms. Due to the solitary nature of my writing work in California, I had lacked fellowship and camaraderie. I had put less energy into building relationships. As such, loneliness played a significant role in my troubles.

I began to make a list of all the things that might be troubling me, calling it my "Sad/Mad Diary." I became what could be called a "psychonaut," an explorer of my own psyche, trying to connect the thread of pain to the offending sadness or anger. "What am I mad about?" I asked. "What am I sad about?" I searched within my heart and mind for cognitive dissonance and internal conflicts, ranging from the stresses of daily life to childhood trauma.

My list swelled to about twenty-five possibilities, which I grouped into categories such as childhood, family, love, career, and health. During psychotherapy sessions, I brought these subconscious gremlins into conscious awareness. My therapist said psychoanalysis was like the work of the digestive tract. Instead of churning up and metabolizing food, psychoanalysis helped break down and process conflicts. Avoiding talks about our troubles could lead to "psychic indigestion," he told me. And that might lead to problems. For some, it's substance abuse, risky behavior, workaholism, or any number of destructive behaviors. In my case, I would somatize, or convert my distress into physical symptoms, much like Crichton did when he was experiencing existential angst about his future.

This level of understanding led to another book, *Anatomy of an Illness: As Perceived by the Patient* by Norman Cousins. Cousins was an editor for Saturday Review who, in 1964, developed a sudden-onset case of the crippling and incurable condition, ankylosing spondylitis. Doctors gave Cousins a one in five hundred chance of recovering. He chronicled his full recovery in his 1979 best seller.

Reflecting on his process of self-healing, Cousins wrote that he took massive intravenous doses of Vitamin C and ate a nutrient-dense diet (versus the highly processed food he was served in the hospital). He was also an advocate of "laughter as the best medicine" and wrote about going on marathon movie-watching sessions composed solely of comedies. "I made the joyous discovery that ten minutes of genuine belly laughter had an anesthetic effect and would give me at least two hours of pain-free sleep. When the pain-killing effect of the laughter wore off, we would switch on the motion picture projector again and not infrequently, it would lead to another pain-free interval."

Perhaps undergoing my own transformation, I wondered if I could maybe write something like Cousins had. I told a physical therapist that I was on a quest to understand the link between my mind and body. She suggested that I stop trying to solve the puzzle. Stop reading and writing. Stop obsessing.

"Maybe you should just move on with your life," she offered.

I knew this invasive, open-heart surgery on my health struggles was blunting my recovery, but I told her that it was in my nature to reflect. I needed to get perspective on what I was now referring to as my "Fight Club Year," referring to the 1999 movie. "I need to tell people what happened and why, so it doesn't happen to them," I said.

I reminded myself that many, if not all, of the symptoms I had considered serious ended up being minor. Even the most worrying symptom had eventually passed. The back pain, in all likelihood, wasn't an incurable autoimmune condition; it was probably tense muscles caused by distress and prolonged sitting. The anal fissure, while excruciating, wasn't colon cancer or Crohn's disease, and it was treatable with a cream, not surgery. A twitching finger wasn't multiple sclerosis but likely came from repetitive strain and an aggravation of the ulnar nerve from long writing sessions. The scaly, cracked skin between my toes wasn't psoriatic arthritis but a diagnosed case of athlete's foot, treated with an antifungal cream.

I was getting clarity, and my imagination started to turn outward to projects and relationships. After a few months of not writing anything creative, I was writing again with vigor. If I felt pain, I examined my emotions, asking myself, "What's bothering me?" or "What is the pain trying to distract me from?" I even started to ignore physical symptoms, robbing them of attention and the fears that fed them. If my finger twitched, my hand ached, or my back hurt, I'd shift my mind to a work project or go for a walk. I noticed that symptoms just went away after several weeks. I listened to my body more. I had spent a year resenting my body for keeping me in pain, a prisoner. Now, I was getting messages to be gentler with myself. As I continued a dialogue with my body, I heard feedback of self-care: "Slow down." "Relax." "Go for a walk."

I applied for a clinical trial at Massachusetts General Hospital that studied how self-compassion affected the brains of people suffering from chronic back pain. The study used neuroimaging to examine the brain's functioning before and after self-compassion training. Through a series of six exercises, our teachers showed us how to direct kindness toward ourselves. During the first activity, I felt as if waves of electricity were radiating throughout my body, as if my nervous system had been plugged into an outlet.

Every day during the month-long trial, I practiced the daily guided self-compassion meditations. I whispered phrases to myself that I had developed in our group training, such as "I am loved, unconditionally," "I am a good man," "I am well," "May I be gentle with myself," "May I slow down," and, most importantly I found, "May I know that I am enough." Sometimes I felt nothing while I whispered these phrases; other times, I felt a flood of emotion, usually sadness. I was tapping into a reservoir of grief that was still embedded in my body, perhaps from my past relationship or tension from constantly searching for a diagnosis, maybe even childhood trauma. All these wounds were getting attention, receiving compassion. Love.

I was making progress, but I was still a stranger to my emotions. I got the chance to practice grief when a short-term romance ended. I burst into tears over coffee. I thought it was a good sign, actually. I was becoming more emotive.

Dr. O'Sullivan writes that many people with psychosomatic symptoms are often recognized as being alexithymic, or unable to interpret their own emotional states. A psychologist said that I probably wasn't alexithymic, but she agreed that I was still suppressing some emotions. Much of my anger, I found, was the result of daily grievances. I realized that we all swallow a lot of crap in life. The car that cuts you off in traffic, the insensitive coworker, or the taking of direction from inept leaders. Usually, we choke down these annoyances and complain to our friends and spouses. I rebelled against that. If I was mad, I swore. If I was sad, I cried. By not suppressing emotions, I felt less bottled up. The anxiety and despair began to fade.

I experimented with alternative treatments, including craniosacral therapy, a healing technique that claims to release myofascial tension and open energy blockages by the triggering of meridians. At the start of my first session, the Chinese therapist placed her hands on my back, stomach, neck, and forehead. Her touch was gentle, nurturing.

"You have a strong body, but there's tension in your shoulders, neck, and lower back," she explained.

She found tightness in my jaw, which could have caused the ringing in my ears, though she said it might have a psychological component too. She moved her hands softly around my body as we discussed pain.

"This is the first time I've ever experienced health issues that are chronic," I said.

She grinned. "Welcome to the war."

"Why would my body continue to send pain signals after the tissues are healed?"

She suggested it could be from my work habits. As a writer, my brain carries my body around: reading, thinking, and writing. "I live from the neck up," I told her.

She said working at a desk all day produces tension in the body and that even ninety minutes of sitting can produce damage. "Maybe the pain is your body's way of getting you to pay attention to it?"

"You think my body just wants to be nurtured?" I asked.

She suggested that I get up from my desk frequently to remind my body that I hadn't forgotten about it. "Give fifty-nine minutes to work and one minute to God."

The conversation became more philosophical.

"I want to *cure* the pain," I said. "How can I do that?"

"Everyone has their own inner physician and their own inner drugstore." She told me that healing completely would require that I activate both.

When I asked how, she encouraged me to start a dialogue with my pain. "Ask the pain what it wants."

I closed my eyes as she worked and asked. I told the therapist that the voice said, "Listen."

"That's a good start."

I shut my eyes and asked my body what it wanted. It said, "Love." I assumed that meant romantic love, as I was lonely.

"Maybe it's your body that wants love," she said. "Give yourself a hug sometime."

She asked if I had experienced failure recently. I told her about my year in California and that I might have suffered a nervous breakdown.

She nodded compassionately. "What about loss?"

I told her about my ex-girlfriend, Paige, and the grief I had only just begun to process.

"Do you have a purpose in life?"

I told her I was a writer. I told stories, hopefully to provide perspective, lift people's spirits, maybe even help them heal.

"A purpose is important." She asked me what I did for fun.

I couldn't remember the last time I'd had fun.

"I think I forgot how to have fun," I said, surprising myself. "I have no joy."

The session ended, but she kept a hand on my back as we talked. Her touch was caring, comforting. "You have a good start because you've accepted the mind-body connection. Most people never get that far. Keep listening to your body; it will give you all the answers."

That night, I wrapped my arms around my chest and gave myself a hug. My eyes welled up with tears. My body whispered back, "Thank you."

After that session, I became radically healthy. I established a sleep schedule, stayed hydrated, did yoga every other day, meditated daily, and stayed social. Yoga was especially helpful; it helped strengthen my back, lower stress, and tame my nervous system. For a few months, I took the weekends off from writing. Open weekends encouraged my mind to play more. I was more mentally flexible and imaginative. This set the stage for creative spurts. I recorded the influx of ideas into my phone. The thoughts became raw material for creative writing projects.

Occasionally, I'd slip back into thinking the back pain was the result of a structural issue. I saw a chiropractor, who thought that, while stress was certainly one component, some of the back pain could have originated from the facet joints in my lower back. He pointed out that the joints were compressed due to a forward tilt of my pelvis, which was a result of tight quadriceps and hip flexors—common among people who sit all day. He performed some spinal manipulations and recommended stretches and exercises that relieved the pressure between the facet joints.

In physical therapy, I strengthened my back and core muscles. I did a full ergonomic revamp of my workspace, adding a keyboard tray, a split keyboard, a vertical mouse, and dictation software for hands-free writing. Every half hour, I got up from my desk and walked. I used an app to meditate three times a day, which helped still my distressed mind. It also helped me change my perception of the pain. I was still in pain, but not suffering as much.

I established a walking routine, using the half hour not for aimless daydreaming or distraction but for deliberate rumination. I would dwell on emotions that were troubling me. I worked out frustrations on these walks. If an intense emotion welled up, I stayed with it and worked through it. I didn't always come to a resolution; the therapeutic value was in consciously acknowledging the feelings.

While I was making progress in physical therapy, I still wasn't sure if I would ever be able to return to vigorous activity. I met with Dr. Zacharia

Isaac, a spine and pain care specialist, coincidently at the hospital for which I worked. He listened intently as I told him about my struggle with back pain. He was confident, authoritative, and thoughtful. I could tell he cared. I told him that I was an athlete and used to do in-home workouts, like P90X. He said that he'd help me get back to P90X. It was a profound statement. His conviction made me believe I might recover, which no other doctor had been able to do.

When we discussed exercise, Dr. Isaac said that most people who experience back pain tend to stop their usual activities, thinking it might make the situation worse. It's called "fear and avoidance," and it's the last thing you want to do, as the core and back muscles can atrophy, providing less support to the spine. It seemed counterintuitive, but I had to stay physically active when I was in pain, *especially* when I was in pain. It was the safest and most effective way to resolve a back-pain episode, according to recently released guidelines from the American College of Physicians.

That night, I performed a thirty-minute dynamic exercise Dr. Isaac had posted on his YouTube page for patients. It was painful but not as bad as I had thought it would be. I was moving again. Meeting with Dr. Isaac gave me hope. He helped me believe that I'd fully recover. It was curious to me that while I had access to the best healthcare and some of the best doctors in the country, it wasn't potent drugs or advanced technology that had started me down the road to recovery; it was empathy and nurturing care.

On Dr. Isaac's suggestion, I took a mindfulness-based stress reduction (MBSR) course in the Greater Boston Area. Developed by Jon Kabat-Zinn, MBSR is a scientifically proven method to reduce anxiety, depression, and pain. In the first class, the teacher told us that it was a dirty little secret in medicine that doctors didn't really want to deal with chronically ill patients because they don't get better and they complain a lot. I could relate.

For my MBSR class, I meditated forty-five minutes a day for eight weeks. My favorite of the guided meditations on CD, which were led by Jon Kabat-Zinn, was the full body scan. The body scan made me realize that I was quite disembodied. For years, my mind had been carrying my body around: dragging it to rugby matches, marathons, and triathlons and pushing it through long writing sessions without its consent. At the end of a body scan meditation, I felt lighter, connected to something expansive.

Many months later, I received a diagnosis from an ear, nose, and throat doctor. Apparently, I had a common condition called laryngopharyngeal reflux (LPR), or silent reflux. LPR is like acid reflux, but the stomach acid irritates the throat, not the esophagus. It's tricky to diagnose because it doesn't cause a burning sensation in many people, including me. It explained why I was waking up in the night gasping. The irritation causes swelling and the buildup of mucus in the throat, so much so that it can narrow and even close while sleeping. I started taking an acid-reducing tablet before dinner, stayed away from certain foods, ate smaller meals, didn't snack before bed, and tried to maintain a healthy weight.

A year after my breakdown in a Californian hospital, I had weaned myself off the antidepressant. I canceled all doctor appointments except those with my therapy. I quit googling symptoms, cold turkey. If an ache or pain crept up, I ignored the urge to research them online. My mind is just too suggestible.

It took many months, but with meditation, medication, yoga, walking and swimming, friendships, romantic relationships, and reflection during therapy sessions, my body released the trauma. I experienced fewer stress responses and became less reactive. My nervous system and immune system stopped overreacting. My biochemistry normalized. The sadness and anger dissolved.

Occasionally, after a poor night of sleep, a vigorous yoga class, or a stressful period at work, I will still experience an ache in my lower back. If this happens, I'll go for a walk, get a massage, or attend a yoga class. If I feel tight or sore, I'll spend twenty minutes in the sauna, stretching. While I may always remain vexed by the exact sources of my mysterious physical symptoms, I no longer have any fear around them. If something hurts, it's almost irrelevant.

A year after returning from California, I was asked by Robert Jamison, Ph.D.—a clinical psychologist with over thirty years of experience working with people who suffer from chronic pain—to talk about my experience dealing with psychosomatic illness with the pain clinic at the hospital for which I worked. As their patient and colleague, I sat at the head of a large conference table and told my story to a roomful of psychologists, physicians, and nurses: I had driven my motorcycle from a small town in New

Hampshire to Los Angeles to follow my dreams as a writer, but reoccurring bouts of back pain soon started me down a road of worry, which led to chronic pain and rheumatological, immunological, and neurological symptoms. Eventually, these led to catastrophizing, insomnia, anxiety, and depression.

To the room full of healthcare providers, I explained how months of reflecting, reading many books on psychosomatic medicine, and listening to sometimes conflicting advice from doctors, I had thought myself into illness and then thought myself out again. I had healed myself by accepting that my physical symptoms didn't have a physical cause, but rather a psychological one. I told them that the major life crisis had stimulated a post-traumatic growth. I was less of a stranger to myself. I was encouraged to accept myself, even love myself. The cure was to face the emotional troubles that my conscious mind was trying so hard to avoid.

I have a scientific way of looking at the world, but I could only muster what felt like a spiritual explanation for my illness. I think the pain was a message. It served a purpose. It slowed me down, got me to listen to my body. It reminded me to stop pushing so hard, to accept myself. In that way, perhaps the pain was a gift.

At my follow-up cranial sacral therapy session, the Chinese therapist didn't recognize me right away. She guessed it had been a year since we last met, but it had only been a couple of months. She said my energy was much calmer.

"Last session, your aura was localized around your head," she said. "Now it's surrounding your body and is radiating outward."

I told her about my recovery. That I swam and did yoga a few times a week. I also had a daily meditation practice, which helped make me less reactive.

As she moved her hands around my body, putting pressure on a point on my palm that supposedly released back pain, we discussed pain again and what it had taught me.

"I think of pain as a teacher," she said.

"In that way, it's almost like a gift."

She nodded knowingly. "It was a message that you were ignoring something."

After the session, I asked if she could recommend a book on craniosacral therapy.

She smiled and said I didn't need another book.

"Feel your body, slow down your mind, and you'll be fine."

CHAPTER 19

A Morning Dose of Awe

For the past several years, I've spent most weekday mornings watching the news while I eat breakfast. At some point, I realized this habit wasn't doing me any favors.

The never-ending churn of stories of murders, disasters, shootings, missing persons, and political missteps, and the commercials about the many ways my body and mind could go haywire had produced a chronic, low-level anxiety. I needed to replace the news with a different morning routine. I wanted a TV show that was enriching, nourishing, something that would calm me down, not rev me up.

When I found the Discovery Channel's *Sunrise Earth* on YouTube, I was spellbound. The nature documentary TV series, which started in 2004, has a simple premise: Put cameras in beautiful geographic locations all over the world—lights go up at dawn. The sixty-four episodes run about fifty minutes and include stunning high-definition videos with titles like Cloud Forest Waterfall, Buddhists of Wat Svay, Yellowstone National Park, Swallow Sea Cave, a Mayan pyramid, and Argentinean Seal Pups.

Refreshingly, there's no narration or music. The show is reality television of the natural world. According to Wikipedia, the genre is "experiential TV," which the TV critic Tom Shales describes as "crazily uneventful and thoroughly wonderful." My first episode was Andean Dawn at Machu Picchu, set in the ancient Incan city in the High Andes. The episode begins in near darkness at 5:14 a.m. in Urubamba, Peru, 8,000 feet above sea level. Shots last about thirty seconds.

The sky is blue gray. Mist swirls around jagged cliffs. Crumbled white granite blocks surround green paths. Birds chirp, hidden creatures squeak, a lama rests alone. There's an expansive hum from the Urubamba River below. Does this magnificent spectacle really happen every day? I was enchanted by the events of this mystical place. In *Sunrise Earth*, I found a morning dose of awe.

What is "awe," though? In an article in *Philosophy Now*, author Robert Clewis cites the psychologists Dacher Keltner and Jonathan Haidt, who wrote that awe "involves a response to something larger than oneself—a perceived vastness—and a need for accommodation, referring to how we make sense of and adjust to what we experience."

Later in the episode, the magical world awakens. The sky has brightened over Machu Picchu, and a massive sun engulfs the screen. In high-definition zoom, a tiny bird perched on a cliff pecks at browning grass. So close to the action, I study the swirls of gray, orange, and red in its feathers.

In his article, Clewis adds that awe is a "complex, mixed feeling of intense satisfaction sensed before a striking or inspiring object, event, or act. It includes the positive feeling of exaltation before a vast or powerful object, such as a natural wonder …"

At 6:15 a.m., the sun has climbed higher. Human visitors trickle into the ancient ruins. The camera holds on an orange-colored plant nurtured by moisture from the cloud forest. A falcon floats on a thermal updraft. A lama yawns, lowers its head to pull grass from the earth. I examine tiny hairs on its cheeks.

I realized that watching *Sunrise Earth* was the morning routine I'd needed. It had given me a much-needed break from the extreme weather, the misconduct, and missing persons. It gave me relief from words like "dangerous" and "terrifying" and "tragic." It provided escape from images of bleeding gums, eroding joints, and overactive immune systems.

But there was another unexpected antidote. "Awe draws attention away from the self and toward the environment," Clewis writes, "and the brain regions associated with self-awareness are deactivated, not activated."

For years, the news was the perfect drug for my conscious mind's endless quest for excitement, but another part of me—call it my soul, perhaps—craved experiences of awe. *Sunrise Earth* gave me a break from the everyday affairs of the world, but it also gave me a break from myself. And maybe that's what I was searching for all along.

CHAPTER 20

The Stick

In the fifteen years I've worked in Corporate America as a writer of marketing copy, my free-spirited father, Greg—a self-employed builder in a sleepy town in northern New Hampshire—has been a fictive vessel for my wishes: to work for myself, to live in a more tranquil, rural setting, to say and do as I please—as he does. While I report to the same building every day, Greg has a different job site every few weeks.

While I attend back-to-back meetings throughout the day, seldom in control of time, Greg plans his schedule and can come and go as he pleases. I do what I'm told, or I'll be shown the door. No one tells my father what to do or how to think. I envy his agency and ability to be an individual when I must remain obedient, present an artificial identity, and avoid sincerity for the sake of civility.

Though I'm ashamed to admit it, I'm similar to Edward Norton in the movie *Fight Club*—and my father is Brad Pitt. It's embarrassing because Norton's character, the narrator of the story, named Jack, is a tense, miserable corporate employee who can't sleep because he's living a mundane, meaningless life. To cope with his gloomy existence, Jack invents a man who helps him fulfill his subconscious desire to live with more confidence. That person is Pitt's character, Tyler Durden. Tyler is everything the narrator admires: confident, charismatic, and, most of all, free to do and say as he pleases.

In the same way the narrator in *Fight Club* put his alter ego, Tyler, on a pedestal, I've put my father above mere mortals. I revere his devil-may-care attitude that allows him to follow his gut when he's lost on a motorcycle trip with friends. When I ride, my destination is set on my phone's GPS, and the route is mapped out before I depart, leaving almost zero room for error. Greg fancies "winging it," whereas I sweat the details. My father sleeps soundly; I wake up at night gasping from acid reflux.

The vanity license plate on his truck reads "GBOGH," meaning "Go Big or Go Home." And he couldn't care less if someone driving behind him can't decipher the acronym.

Three-quarters of the way through *Fight Club*, Jack realizes that he's spent months split from reality, communicating with a person who's never been there. Just before he passes out, overwhelmed by the depth of his psychosis, Tyler explains why Jack invented him:

> All the ways you wish you could be, that's me. I look like you wanna look, I f*** like you wanna f***, I am smart, capable, and most importantly, I'm free in all the ways that you are not.

Like Jack did with Tyler, I idealize my father and his attitude of not giving a f***. But there's a problem with idealization: it's built on a foundation of denial. It often means that you're revering a person, idea, worldview—anything, in fact—without acknowledging its negative aspects.

Idealization is not believing reality; it's seeing the good without the bad.

For instance, Tyler is charming and bold but also chaotic and violent. He's someone to marvel at for his gumption but also to dread for his recklessness. He's clever but also juvenile. A role model and a criminal. Was the same dynamic at play with my father? What negative aspects of him was I denying?

I realized that by idealizing Greg, I could overlook his faults. My idealized father leads his friends down an unknown trail while mountain biking, but my real father must admit he's taken a wrong turn. My idealized father dashes off unreadable emails to business clients, but my real father loses potential income when those clients cut ties over his lack of professionalism. My idealized father preaches the gospel of self-reliance, but my real father has trouble connecting with people because he often chooses to ignore their pain and dispenses advice instead.

Why do I need this fictionalized version of Greg? By keeping him on a pedestal, I can deny my anger toward him. For years, I've viewed him and his lifestyle through rose-tinted glasses while being seriously, albeit subconsciously, angry at him. Greg was of a generation that saw corporal punishment as appropriate disciplinary action. His father hit him with belts, sticks, and coat hangers. His grandfather probably did the same. In childhood, if my brother or I did something reckless, like dropping small boulders down the well in our yard to hear the splash, not knowing we were destroying its inner workings and costing hundreds, we were given a whipping.

As a young boy, I was terrified of how my father would discipline us with a short piece of wood he kept atop the refrigerator and fetched if we acted out. If we were disobedient or broke the rules, we'd scatter and look for hiding places as Greg jogged to the refrigerator to retrieve The Stick. My brother might have slid underneath his bed, and I would entomb myself in a closet behind hanging shirts. My father always found us, however, and dragged us out by an arm or a leg and smacked us on the rear end as we writhed, covered our faces, and wailed.

Jack invented Tyler to rebel against his meaningless life; I created an unrealistic version of my father to ignore my adolescent rage. By idealizing Greg as the ultimate free spirit, I avoided my anger for the pain he caused when I was a child. It meant not accepting that being dominated, hit repeatedly, and left squirming on the floor in pain had been humiliating. Idealizing my father helped me repress the terror of his pursuit with the intent of using The Stick on me. I wouldn't have to accept that such events made me an anxious adult who still has shame buried in the dark corners of my body.

While Jack starts off the film as cynical, depressed, and psychotic, he's victorious across the story as a whole, in several ways. He quits his soul-deadening job, starts a cultural movement—a cult, basically, and finds a woman who darkly complements him. Jack's biggest achievement, in my opinion, is that he finally pierces his illusions and, in doing so, discovers his authentic self. He does so by retracing Tyler's steps to learn that the man who's been disrupting his life is, in fact, his own split personality.

I, too, have climbed out of denial by accepting that the fictional version of my father isn't real but rather a figment of my imagination—the same way that Tyler was for the narrator. I've ceased putting Greg on a pedestal and stopped telling people that his harsh disciplinary style gave my brother and me the enviable self-discipline we have today. Like Jack, I must continue to summon the courage to confront reality and stare clear-eyed into the facts of my life. The truth is that I suffered through trauma and should be kind to myself while the psychic wounds heal.

Near the end of *Fight Club*, Jack realizes that by not idealizing Tyler, he's left only with himself—a product of all the desperation, psychosis, and pain he's experienced. Not worshiping my father lets me see that he's like all of us: flawed but just doing the best he can. In place of that idealization, I can find something else: admiration. I value his positive qualities and accept his negative, all-too-human ones. He's a go-getter, but restless. A problem-solver, but unreflective. An optimist, but intolerant of negative views.

Getting honest about Greg allowed me to get real about myself. I had to stop denying that authoritarian managers at work were making me unhappy. So when I was offered a new copywriting job for an audio engineering company, I resigned. In my new role, I still write within a corporate environment, but the organization is less bureaucratic and hierarchical and open to fresh ideas. I work in a "storytelling pod" with a team of talented creatives who are funny, open-minded, and laid-back. It's a good fit, and I've flourished. And the melancholy and restlessness have lifted.

At the end of *Fight Club*, Jack realizes he doesn't need the alter ego to cope anymore. When Tyler refuses to leave, Jack puts a gun in his mouth and threatens to shoot. Just before he pulls the trigger, Jack looks into the eyes of his idealized self and says, "Tyler … My eyes are open." When he shoots, the bullet bloodies his face and knocks his jaw out of place, but it doesn't fatally wound him. The bullet does, however, kill Tyler, who blows out a whisper of smoke, drops to his knees, and dies. Not a physical death, but a symbolic one. Jack killed his alter ego.

Like Jack, I, too, have laid the fictionalized version of Greg to rest. By accepting my reality, I admit that I'm not my father—nor do I want to be. I don't live in the woods; I'm a city dweller. I'm not self-employed; I work in Corporate America. I'm not carefree; I'm careful. When making choices, I don't think about Greg's values; I consult my own. With the idealized version gone, only my real father is left, warts and all.

And by opening my eyes, at last, I have discovered myself.

CHAPTER 21

How to Fix a Bluey Heart

By my mid-thirties, most of my college friends had moved out of Boston to other cities. Many were married and starting families. While they bought homes and built families, I focused my time and energy on writing essays and fiction, trying to become the best writer I could be. I wasn't making many new friendships, and I didn't often see the friends I had. Devoting all my spare time to pursuing my goals, I dated casually, avoiding commitment. These were productive years, but I was disconnected and lonely.

Tragically, I didn't see a problem with this dynamic. Not only had I forgotten the value of friendship—once asking a psychologist to "sell me on friendship"—but I also thought my happiness didn't depend on others. This attitude came from growing up with my father and brother in a hyper-masculine household. In my father's home, a "real man" is self-reliant. A "real man" pursues his goals without help from others. A "real man" doesn't need support from friends or loved ones. If you're dependent, you're vulnerable, and a "real man" is never vulnerable. It took me years to realize that this was bullshit. Now I know that everyone needs care and support to flourish in life—yes, even men. Without nurturing, without love, we can wither. And I had been withering.

When I met Sam at 35, I still wasn't sure what I wanted from a romantic relationship—to marry, build a family, live in the suburbs—but I knew what I needed. Casual dating had run its course, providing less and less fulfillment. I knew I needed someone who could satisfy my emotional needs, not my sexual desires. I needed someone to offer support. Someone to listen to me and validate my ideas. I needed someone to care.

Sam and I met in Boston, at an MFA program in creative writing. We hit it off right away at one of our program's ten-day residencies, where all the students came to campus for workshops, classes, readings, and more.

Since then, we've been inseparable. Together, we have visited beaches, parks, and bars all over New England and beyond. We edit each other's work. We've met each other's families. We constantly joke and laugh. Early on, I realized that Sam was the best friend I desperately needed.

We're perhaps an odd pairing. I was in my mid-thirties from the mountains of New Hampshire, living in Boston at the time. She was in her late twenties from the beaches of Florida and had been living in New York City at the time. I studied science, she studied theater. I write science fiction, she writes young adult. But we're similar in many ways. We both grew up lower-class. We both see the world's absurdity and mock it. And we're both writers—hungry to find our voices and make our marks on the world.

A preschool teacher at the time, Sam has the unique gift of being able to comfort tiny humans who can't always tell her where it hurts. It's a superpower she often uses on me. If I'm stressed or frustrated, Sam senses it. She listens to me when I'm disappointed. She tolerates me when I'm mad. And she does all of this without my asking for help from her. This is important because—due to my upbringing—I never ask.

Though I was already working on it in therapy, Sam was unwittingly helping me reform my decidedly "jock" origins. Regrettably, in high school and college, I displayed a fair share of toxic masculinity. A "never show weakness" attitude in the halls and classroom. Ignorant jokes in locker rooms. Tough-guy behavior with friends. Anything else was wimpy or weak.

To be fair, my interpretation of masculinity was like most of the males who came of age in my generation. A man of my era never showed softness. A man of this time didn't admit fault. A man of this time didn't ask for directions if they took a wrong turn. We were adept at pushing away emotions and soldiering on during tough times. Therapy helped me unlearn this programming. But women also played a large part in my reeducation—working with them, loving them, sometimes hating them. Yet, it was Sam's caring and nurturing that allowed me to drop the macho facade and be vulnerable, thereby helping me build a less repressed, more sincere view of myself and manhood.

It wasn't just my father who had predisposed me to having a troubled relationship with my emotions. During childhood, my mother could be emotionally distant and wasn't adept at understanding my emotional needs.

When I was upset, she struggled to understand the cause of my distress and didn't always know how to take away the pain. I don't blame her because it wasn't entirely her fault. I've always sensed that my mother doesn't quite know how to label her own emotions and console herself when she's distressed. Instead, she avoids vulnerability and talking about her feelings, and often busies herself in a distracting activity. I also knew that in her teenage years, my mother went through a traumatic event that drove her further away from her own feelings. And so, in addition to inheriting my father's macho attitude, I got my mother's habit of avoiding emotions, negative ones in particular.

It was Sam who helped me overcome this tragic handicap. First, she tunes into my emotional state. Then she gives me the nurturing I am too afraid to—or don't know how to—request. She then holds space for me to be vulnerable—a medicine my parents didn't seem to have.

To help illustrate Sam's powers, it's best to show how she works with children. Once, Sam was babysitting an adorable 6-year-old who had grown upset when her parents had to work longer than usual in the midst of the Coronavirus Pandemic. Sam could tell that the little girl was feeling ignored. Knowing this "sweet little nugget just needed some lovin'," Sam delivered a prescription of snuggles while the child wept in her lap and explained why she was sad. An hour later, they were on the playground, and the nugget was crossing the monkey bars with confidence.

This is Sam's gift, and it's been working its magic on me since we met. Her secret could be called "extreme empathy." For better or worse, she feels everyone's pain and is often willing to take it on to help. One of Sam's favorite books to read to her students is *The Giving Tree* by Shel Silverstein. She relates to the apple tree in the story that gives a little boy everything he needs while he grows older. Over the course of the boy's life, the tree gives the boy parts of itself—apples, branches, and its trunk to make a boat—until the tree eventually becomes a stump. The boy returns to the tree as an old man. Only a stump by this point, the tree can only offer the man a seat. "The tree was happy."

Like the *Giving Tree*, Sam often feels that she gives pieces of herself to others to relieve their suffering. When Sam wakes up in the middle of the night, more often than not, it's because of her extreme empathy flaring up.

Worrying about others, she sympathizes with a problem I'm having, thinks about how she can help her struggling younger sister, or how scared her students are at having to go back to school during the pandemic.

Like the *Giving Tree*, Sam gives pieces of herself to the people in her life and lets them empty themselves out in her presence. It's what she did with that child she was babysitting, and it's what she's done with me many times. Sam lets you vent if you're frustrated or pout when you're down. With her, I can share an insight from therapy, an idea for a story, or a dream I had the night before. And when I empty myself, I feel full.

Early on, as we got to know each other, I told Sam about my previous long-term relationship I'd had with a woman I've been calling Paige. With Paige, I felt like a lottery winner. I had found someone who satisfied my emotional needs and my desires for sexual fulfillment. We'd broken up six years prior, and I told Sam that my heart had been "bluey" ever since.

I had been dating casually but was emotionally unavailable for romantic partners. I had also developed the unfortunate pattern of looking for sexual fulfillment from women who I knew wouldn't satisfy my emotional needs. It's a painful trick I often play on myself. If I pursue someone who's a poor fit, the relationship will ultimately fail. And when it fails, I don't get hurt because I knew it would never work anyway.

Sam helped me patch up my bluey heart.

Spending time with Sam helped me realize that I hadn't been reflecting on my relationship with Paige accurately. Comparing Paige to Sam, I had overestimated how intimate I'd been with Paige. Paige wasn't as attuned to my emotional needs as I had thought. The night before she moved to the west coast, we attended a Red Sox game. Distraught over her departure, I broke into tears on the subway on the ride home. Paige rubbed my back awkwardly, not knowing how to comfort me, as my mother might have done when I was a boy. Also, in looking back, Paige wasn't much interested in my writing goals either. To be fair, it's not that she didn't care at all about my dreams. Rather, she was in her mid-twenties and didn't have the bandwidth to focus on my self-discovery and evolution because she was learning and developing who she was at the same time.

As I spent more time with Sam, the loneliness and disconnection I had been feeling began to lift. It was a tremendous boost for me to talk about writing with Sam. Together, we stoked the fires of each other's passion for the craft. We listened to each other's ideas, helped nurture them into reality, and read and edited each other's work. It's not uncommon for one of us to text the other about a compelling premise for a story and then send a screenshot the next morning of the first page we'd written. Sam was my sounding board for story or article ideas.

With more attention and dialogue around my passion, the quality of my work began to improve. So powerful was having someone interested in my ideas, it gave me the confidence to take creative risks in my work. During my MFA, I changed my style of fiction from a commercial to a more literary style—from Dan Brown to Edgar Allen Poe. My writing went to another level, and publishing opportunities started to roll in.

Meanwhile, if I ever became frustrated or confused, Sam held space for me to be vulnerable. It was the first time I'd ever relied on someone, and it felt good to be supported. When my head is in the clouds, musing over concepts or philosophizing over theories, I can neglect the mundane tasks of daily living. If I'm preoccupied, Sam steps in to remind me to update my iPhone. She'll grab a broom and sweep the floor if it's been neglected. She'll help diagnose a computer issue if it's driving me crazy. If I have a demanding workday approaching, Sam will deliver an iced coffee to my apartment.

In therapy, I continued to explore my failed relationship with Paige. It took a while, but at last, I figured out why our breakup had destroyed me.

When I was about five, my mother left our family for a year or so, which confused my younger brother and me. For us, it was the incomprehensible nature of her leaving that was most traumatic. Another inexplicable loss occurred when my grandmother died of cancer when I was seventeen, which re-triggered the loss of my mother in me. So when Paige moved across the country, I once again felt abandoned by a woman for reasons I couldn't grasp. But I knew Sam wasn't going to leave, and that was good medicine for a bluey heart like mine. I once asked Sam where she thought she'd be in five years. "Wherever you are," she said.

Over time, I recognized that though I had loved Paige, we met at the wrong time in our lives. I knew that if I didn't follow her to the Pacific Northwest, I would lose her. And I did lose her. Selfish as it may seem,

I didn't follow her because I needed that time to focus on my writing. A young artist needed time—years of intense study. Misguided or not, I felt if I didn't give everything to the craft in my thirties, I'd never become who I wanted to become. Again, perhaps this is self-centered, but writing gives meaning to my life and I've made sacrifices for it. I sacrificed someone I loved.

Two years into meeting Sam, I got the closure I needed with Paige. I got in touch with Paige and apologized for not moving across the country with her. She expressed her regret as well. She admitted that she knew I needed that time and that she wouldn't be able to fulfill that supportive role that was essential to me. She needed that time to transition as well—to continue learning and understanding who she was and find her place in the world.

The medicine for trauma isn't just talking, reflecting, and shedding cathartic tears. It's also humor. Sam can be lighthearted and playful, and she sometimes giggles at my "serious" ideas about life and death. Without invalidating my ideas, Sam can make light of my criticisms about mindless careerism, the irresponsibility of the media, and the shortness of life. When Sam pokes fun at my seriousness, it lightens me. It reminds me to stop thinking about life and focus on living it. I became sillier and more fun-loving, especially with Sam. I'm still just as dedicated to my work, but I take the journey less seriously now. Thanks to Sam, I take *myself* less seriously.

Now, I would be remiss without revealing that Sam loves me deeply. The love and affection that Sam shows me pales in comparison to anything I've experienced in previous relationships. Her love is so intense, it can't be avoided or denied. And I love her, too. But are we "together"? Are we dating? It's the question everyone asks. It's a constant hum in the background of our companionship. I often think of Sam as my best friend, but she's much more than that.

In the beginning, Sam expressed her desire for physical intimacy, but I'd been holding that part of our relationship back. It wasn't just that Sam doesn't quite fit my "type," which motivates how I choose sexual partners; it was that our relationship provided something more vital to me. I wasn't opposed to the possibility of these desires developing, but when they didn't, I started to believe that we could continue our unique dynamic forever.

Who cares if we weren't officially "boyfriend and girlfriend"? Given how emotionally satisfying our connection is, I could do without the erotic part.

Eventually, this logic broke down. I went on dates with other women and concealed them from Sam. Even though Sam and I aren't in a "relationship," I felt disloyal when seeing other women. Whatever dating I did was short-lived, anyway. I always came back to Sam because I enjoyed her company the most. I have the most fun with her. I'm most fulfilled by her. I love her. And so, I stopped going on dates.

But this decision still didn't address Sam's desires. So, I tackled that conflict by doing what Sam always gives me space to do: be emotionally vulnerable, a skill that took me years to learn and one that all men would be wise to learn in the Twenty-First Century. I divulged that I cherished our connection and intimacy but was still uncertain about my desire for sexual fulfillment. I told her that our deep emotional connection is more important than the passing pleasures of physical intimacy, at least for now. I questioned whether our connection needed to be defined. Could we just keep caring and supporting each other without a label?

During this conversation, I confessed that meeting her was one of the best things that had ever happened to me. I said that she had helped dissolve the disconnection that had found its way into my life in my thirties. I cherished the fact that she watched out for me and wanted the best for me. I had found someone I could laugh with, write with, and go on adventures with.

I had thought I won the lottery with Paige, but I struck gold with Sam. Meeting Sam helped me realize what was missing in my relationship with Paige. I was broken after Paige, and Sam helped put me back together. Sam fixed my bluey heart. Now I know how to love again, and, in doing so, how to live again.

CHAPTER 22

Corporate Disobedience

Lydia, vice president of marketing, looked dead serious as she laid a piece of paper on the desk in front of me and tapped it with one finger.

"This email you sent out a few days ago is not how we communicate in a professional setting. To be fully transparent, no one in HR is happy with you right now."

Lydia showed me printouts of responses from the HR professionals whose feathers I'd severely ruffled. Apparently, they hadn't seen anything like my message in their decades-long careers.

My email was a sarcastic response to a heavy-handed email I'd received from a professional in HR who managed training videos instructing personnel how to behave within the hospital for which I worked. She insisted I complete a mandatory training course *that day*—"this needs to be prioritized for completion today"—as she had to submit data to the state the following day.

I was extremely busy at the time, stressed over my workload, but I begrudgingly completed the online training. Then I wrote a sarcastic response describing how I'd climbed Mount Kilimanjaro, run the Paris Marathon, and ridden a motorcycle across the country—yet completing this "enriching, life-affirming training" had become my most cherished accomplishment. I gushed about my desire to frame the new certificate (yes, I was emailed a certificate) and proudly and prominently display it in my apartment.

"With warm wishes," I ended the message.

I suspected the email would get me in trouble, but I wrote it as a form of protest—a kind of corporate disobedience—to get everyone talking about how asinine the trainings were.

The email went viral in the HR department. My words quickly found their way to Lydia, who called this meeting to "check in." She also invited our recently hired creative director, Max, whom I hadn't even met yet. It felt like an attempt to discredit me before I had a chance to prove my worth.

Max was quiet for most of the meeting, observing the interaction.

"These yearly training videos take several hours to finish and trigger angst in our department," I said, defending myself. "They make everyone miserable, and we all complain about them at our desks, but nobody speaks up or does anything about it."

"They're mandatory," Lydia stated.

"But most of the trainings aren't even relevant to our department," I added. "We seldom set foot in the hospital. Can't our department be exempted from irrelevant courses?"

That argument went nowhere, and Lydia suggested I send an apology email, which I later did.

After the meeting, Max called me into his office, hoping to get acquainted with one of his department's writers outside of the disciplinary action.

"I agree the email from HR had an overbearing tone," he said. "And no one likes the training sessions, but everyone does them and just moves on."

"Don't you think someone should speak up?"

Max sighed. "You sent an email that everyone wants to send but never does."

I sensed he admired my boldness—not because it was heroic but because I'd defied socially acceptable behavior to tell it like it is.

In my work life, I'm usually well-liked by most colleagues. A team player, I pitch in when help is needed. I go above and beyond on projects and try to maintain a positive attitude. In other words, I'm a rockstar at work. At least, I was until a major restructuring took place in the marketing department of the hospital.

During the shake-up, the hero in me died. I became a critic with a bad attitude, a rebel who called people out on their bullshit. I became an antihero.

Throughout the "workforce reduction"—as silver-tongued executives refer to mass terminations—fear was palpable. To avoid being fired, several senior employees took early retirement packages while others left for new jobs. Management laid off several people, including the marketing team's senior leadership. I managed to keep my job because I had proven my value as a writer. I considered leaving, but I enjoyed writing about medicine and found interviewing doctors and patients fascinating.

In the downsizing process, several of the hospital's communication departments—including marketing, the website-management team, internal communications, and public relations—were combined into a single department. The new leader had headed the public relations team. Norah, confident, edgy, and cool, intimidated most people. One guy's hands shook when she gave him orders. I got along with her because I didn't suck up to her like others did, and we could joke when the team went out for drinks. Some saw Norah as cold and calculating, a pro-social psychopath. Whether that was true or not, I sensed she wanted to build a great team.

Every week during staff meetings, Norah presented the new department's organizational chart as a game of "fill the open positions." The graphic she displayed on the large TV screen at the front of the room would show a top-down hierarchy of roles and responsibilities. At the top was Norah. As a lowly marketing writer, I was near the bottom of the evolving chain of command. While Norah no doubt thought it useful to regularly present the org chart to her new department—so we could visualize the new team members we needed to hire—displaying the matrix to the anxious group reinforced an inflexible, hierarchical culture in which power was unevenly distributed.

Several months into the rebuild, Norah poached a seasoned marketing executive, Lydia, from a nearby hospital. Joining us, Lydia brought along two of her top lieutenants from her previous employer. This trio of hotshot marketers was given the herculean task of enhancing the hospital's brand, increasing patient volume across the medical specialties, and tracking patients' journeys through the system using sophisticated analytics. The tacticians were assembly-line efficient and swiftly built a small army of marketing managers around them. The team became a tight-knit bunch and created their own subculture within the department, with their own team-building meetings and second Christmas parties. In meetings, they left people cold with ambiguous rhetoric laced with corporate jargon. Skilled in bureaucratic jujitsu, they never broke rank and always covered their asses.

It didn't take long for me to recognize the authoritarian tendencies of Lydia and her team. The marketing team demanded obedience without question, even if it might be impossible to do what they demanded in the given time frame. They adjusted their own deadlines as necessary, but no one else enjoyed the same flexibility. They championed their own ideas and looked at those of others with suspicion. If a project went amiss, they scapegoated the most vulnerable, often professionals like me who had built the creative products in question. When not occupied with their tasks, they busied themselves with mind-numbing conversations about babies, barbecues, and ball games.

In short order, Lydia found me a thorn in her side because of my free thinking and compulsion for honesty. In meetings to kick off new projects, I would propose that directives or deadlines were unrealistic or suggest approaches to accommodate realistic problems that were certain to arise. But even a minor departure from the original vision was interpreted as insubordination.

Lydia and her team weren't impressed by my avant-garde style creativity or my desire to push the boundaries of corporate storytelling using techniques borrowed from journalism and sometimes fiction. Despite my portfolio—hundreds of written pieces for the hospital over two years, a popular medical mysteries column for the health blog, and a video about the Hippocratic oath that earned over sixteen thousand views on YouTube—Lydia and others had little interest in my "big ideas." They couldn't fathom why I refused to uncritically submit to her and other authority figures.

As I worked on a tsunami of projects—which mostly involved writing websites to lure patients into the hospital's web of medical services—I continued observing Lydia and the ice-cold mechanism that was her team. I was shocked to see them bending the truth with regularity. It started with little tricks, like bolstering the marketing team's credibility in meetings with physicians by referring to me as a "senior" writer, despite my having no such title.

Their reality distortion quickly grew more egregious. When the department's office space could no longer hold the growing team, I was offered a cubicle.

"I think I'd rather stay where I am, closer to work friends," I responded.

But it soon became clear that I had no choice. In the next staff meeting, Lydia discussed the building of the cubicles. "Thank you to Dustin and Meghan for graciously agreeing to move into the cubicles."

"Bullshit," I whispered, though no one heard.

As a creative writer in a profit-driven business environment, I regularly found myself in thorny situations. Most of the time, I was focused on writing articles about health conditions for the general public and medical innovations for clinicians. The stakeholders were the marketing professionals who assigned the projects and the clinicians and other experts I interviewed for research and quotes. If a project didn't go as planned, I was often criticized despite my attempt to please all parties.

For example, when a project fell behind schedule, it was me who should have started earlier, not the marketing managers who had assigned the project. If a story didn't include a required marketing message, I should have known it was needed even if no one had told me.

While we creatives—writers, graphic designers, and video producers—were regularly scapegoated, Lydia and her team operated with impunity if problems arose. They worked at their own pace and rearranged deadlines at will. They were uncompromising toward others yet demanded flexibility for themselves. If a mistake was made, someone else must have made it; Lydia's team was above reproach.

As the deceptions piled up, I felt like a young Che Guevara as portrayed in the film *The Motorcycle Diaries*. After a year of travel in South America, during which Guevara witnesses inequality and great human suffering, he refuses to return to his normal life, instead taking his first steps toward the revolutionary he would later become. At the end of the movie, Guevara tells his friend, "So much injustice."

The words resonated with me. I felt like someone needed to say something about the hypocrisy in my department. While the antihero Guevara would choose bullets, my weapons were words.

In our first company retreat as a new department, everyone was asked to share two words: one they felt described the former year and one to describe the year ahead. Given the restructuring, most people alluded to the prior year as being stressful and the year ahead as hopeful.

At my turn, I said, "Before I share my two words, I want to mention the four stages of the creative process: preparation, incubation, illumination, and implementation."

"Here comes a thesis," Norah said sarcastically.

My intent wasn't to sound clever; I just wanted to provide context for my two words: *illumination* (the process of trying to understand the business problems that need solving) and *implementation* (the start of campaigns to resolve the problems).

"This is why you're a problem for me," Norah said.

I laughed uncomfortably. I had a reputation for sharing "deep thoughts," often through the lens of psychology or philosophy. Some people admired me for stating aloud what others might be thinking, but discussing truths so openly could make others uncomfortable, especially in tight-lipped settings like our office.

Until then, however, I hadn't realized I was a "problem" for Norah. I had thought we got along well. I had assumed the marketing team talked about me behind closed doors and not with others.

This was likely a result of Norah's unique management style. Each quarter, Norah met with every employee in the department. These check-ins were an opportunity for us to talk about ourselves and express any concerns we had. In one of my quarterly meetings, I had informed Norah that our department might have a "culture problem."

"I think Lydia and her team have created a subculture that isn't meshing well with the other teams."

"Can you give me any examples?" Norah asked.

"The marketing team can be oppressive with their demands, and some have referred to it as a subtle form of bullying."

"It sounds like a psychologically unsafe environment for people."

"Yes, especially for critical thinkers," I said. "The people who seem to fit in with our evolving department are those who maintain a sheep-like passivity and say yes to anything that leaves Lydia's mouth."

I wasn't sure Norah had ever received such unvarnished truth. In any case, the conversation led to action.

Minutes after the meeting, Norah called Lydia to relay my observations. Lydia quickly scheduled a meeting with her team, who denied any such problem existed. Instead, they scapegoated writers like me.

"It's strange to have them sit in the same area of the office as the marketing team when they're technically part of the content team, not marketing."

The denial from Lydia's group didn't surprise me, as it was Lydia's team that was causing the issue.

While I used my quarterly meetings to provide useful feedback and potentially solve cultural problems in my department, I got the sense that other employees were informing on each other in theirs. In these check-ins, Norah would ask about our jobs, career goals, and lives, but she also rummaged for potential interpersonal conflicts that might require her intervention. While this was intended to head off small problems before they became big ones, it also sowed paranoia into the fabric of the department.

For example, she might ask, "How do you like working with Max?" The reputations of employees could be made or damaged with questions like these. It was in a quarterly meeting with one of my coworkers that Norah learned that I "thought outside the box"—and not in a good way—and that I was prone to dissent.

A quarterly meeting was where Norah learned of the email I'd written to HR. She was also informed I had written a frustrated email—a "nastygram," as she called it—to a marketing manager who had demanded I take on a massive writing project on an impossibly tight deadline on top of an already heavy workload. Norah had been given no context. We had just lost a writer, and I was picking up that person's responsibilities. To make matters worse, during the restructuring, Norah and Lydia had fired the employee who had once managed incoming and outgoing assignments. Now the other writers and I were swamped, with nobody to defend our workloads. In an act of self-preservation, I had objected to the request.

"When do you suppose I will have time for this project?"

I never received a response to my email.

Instead, the marketing manager forwarded the email to Lydia, who then slapped me on the wrist in my performance review. Instead of "lashing out" via email, Lydia explained to me in a robotic tone—undoubtedly honed during her decades of climbing ladders at advertising agencies—the issue should've been brought up with my manager.

"But you fired that person," I clarified.

Lydia said nothing.

"Also, we writers are overwhelmed, and the project request from your marketing manager was oppressive in its tone."

Lydia's allegiance stood with the offended teammate, however, and the context I provided fell on deaf ears. Ultimately, the only reason I wasn't fired over my emails was that I provided value in my role.

Matters moved from bad to worse when Jane was hired as the new content manager—my boss. During the application process, I opposed hiring Jane. On reviewing her writing portfolio, I thought she was a mediocre writer. Jane could inform readers, but in my opinion, she couldn't persuade them or excite them and eventually convert them. In her interview, I found her as dull as a W-2. And though I couldn't put my finger on why, I sensed she played well with others in public but could perhaps be unpleasant when no one was looking. However, she seemed drawn to subjects that the marketing team adored: babies, barbecues, and ball games.

From her first day, Jane nitpicked trivialities in everything I wrote, from articles to video scripts. Almost reflexively, she disregarded my creative ideas, such as a hospital-wide podcast about case studies that I thought would excite the public. For a creative person like me, Jane's indifference was invalidating and more upsetting than outright rejection.

I soon realized that, for Jane, creative professionals who "think different," in the Apple sense of the expression, were insubordinate and disrespectful. And while Jane was quick to disregard my ideas, she seldom had original ones of her own. Instead, she was vulnerable to groupthink in meetings and agreed with others when it was politically expedient or when she sensed a majority opinion developing. And Jane was blindly submissive to Lydia's team, conforming to their every whim.

Of course, the marketing team adored her.

In Lydia's eyes, Jane was managing incoming and outgoing projects adeptly. In my view, however, there was more to managing projects than controlling their flow. Like most employees, I wanted to feel that I was contributing to the team in meaningful ways, but with every project, Jane was thankless and made me feel underappreciated.

A few months into Jane's tenure, the other two writers departed suddenly—one was escorted from the building while screaming at Jane. Now the only writer, I had to pick up most of their responsibilities.

Often, Jane's management style was not only soulless but punitive. For example, I would sometimes submit first drafts of articles that were deliberately too long so stakeholders could review what I'd uncovered in my research and interviews with doctors and patients; I would then edit the article to suit its marketing purposes. But Jane was having none of this.

"You were instructed to stick to the intended word count," she would write in an email, indicating her instructions had been ignored. Worse, Jane used punishing terms in her feedback, such as announcing that marketing had been sending her "complaints" about my articles being too long. *Complaints* is a strong word, I would think. It made me feel like a deviant when I was just trying to help. Jane constantly searched for examples of misconduct and made it her mission to correct any aberrant activity before it became "a pattern."

When the Coronavirus Pandemic hit, the department began working remotely, relying on emails and Zoom calls. As the pandemic raged, Lydia and her team kept their foot on the gas pedal. They gave Jane and me an unprecedented workload—the biggest and most time-consuming projects we'd ever been asked to do in the shortest time ever, all while being understaffed by two writers. None of this appeared to factor into Lydia's decision-making. Neither did the fear, the uncertainty, nor the collective trauma everyone was experiencing in the spreading shadow of the global health crisis.

Under pressure to interview physicians and write several articles quickly, I was trading fiery emails with Jane when it became clear my past "crimes" would haunt me forever. I learned that during the first weeks of Jane's tenure, Lydia and others on the marketing team had waged a smear campaign against me. They had informed Jane about my history of writing sarcastic, unprofessional "knee-jerk" emails. Such perception emboldened Jane to try to keep me in line.

In one venomous email, Jane let slip that she intended to "rehabilitate" me—a phrase so dystopian that it chilled my blood. From what I could tell, Jane's rehabilitation campaign involved making sure I colored within the lines on every project and did what Lydia and the marketing team wanted in the exact ways specified. Jane did all this to the best of her ability, but she did it covertly, relying on emails to put me in my place.

In one instance, I messaged our office manager to reschedule a quarterly meeting with Norah, something I'd done several times since the restructuring. Out of nowhere, Jane emailed the office manager, cc'ing me, to apologize for the hassle I'd caused. This baffled me because the meeting had nothing to do with my supervisor, and rescheduling it was no trouble for the office manager, as she told me later.

The longer I worked with Jane, the more flummoxed I became by my inability to communicate with her. Talking with Jane was like talking to Nurse Ratched from *One Flew Over the Cuckoo's Nest*. In the film, Randle Patrick McMurphy, played by Jack Nicholson, is transferred from a prison farm to the psychiatric ward of a mental institution. McMurphy assumes he can coast his way through his sentence as a mental patient. However, he soon discovers that the ward is run by an all-powerful force—the story's antagonist, Nurse Ratched, played by Louise Fletcher, who controls the patients with rules, medication, and electroconvulsive therapy.

During one of their first encounters, McMurphy asks Nurse Ratched if she can lower the volume of the music in the psychiatric ward. Displaying a cold, insensitive demeanor, Nurse Ratched explains that the music is set to its current volume because some patients have hearing problems. She makes it clear that the matter is nonnegotiable and she won't tolerate him questioning the rule—or any rule.

Her reaction invalidates McMurphy's position, as though he were acting out in anger instead of making a simple request. And what does an invalidating environment controlled by an inflexible, possibly sadistic person like Nurse Ratched do to a rational person? It drives them to rebel, as happened with McMurphy.

A similar dynamic was at play between Jane and me. If I said the scope of a project was too large for the proposed deadline, she would imply I worked too slowly or I wasn't a team player. When I became frustrated because I had too many assignments and not enough time to do them, Jane would write in an email that I was dramatic and unprofessional.

A year into Jane's tenure, she told me I had three days—which included a Saturday and a Sunday—to finish an article about the long-term effects of COVID-19. I told her it was impossible. While I'd already interviewed four physicians for the article, I still had three more to talk to.

"The remaining doctors might not be available for interviews," I explained over a Zoom call.

"I cannot budge on the deadline," was Jane's response.

Since she wouldn't even acknowledge my concerns, I lost my patience. Mockingly, I clapped my hands together once. "Okay, Jane!"

She silently scribbled in her notebook, then coldly said, "Your outburst has been noted." Afterward, she called HR.

At the end of our next meeting, Jane announced, "I wish I didn't have to do this, but I've been told to issue you a verbal warning for your actions."

After the meeting, she emailed me an HR document listing prior transgressions, including my anger over the cubicle incident and the nastygrams I seemed prone to sending. The document also explained how to act in a professional setting.

I felt defeated, confused, and on the verge of tears.

Before working with Lydia, her marketing team, and Jane, I'd always been a nice guy, a team player, and was well-liked around the office. Now, I was the asshole. The bad guy. An antihero.

I realized that once people branded me as having a problem with authority, I would always be dysfunctional in their eyes, particularly those who guarded the prevailing order. At best, bureaucrats like Lydia and Jane would spend their time and energy ensuring that any dissenters always played by the rules. At worst, they would punish them through marginalization, ridicule, even termination. They might even psychopathologize, labeling dissenters like me with anger problems or personality disorders. For example, when someone doesn't play by the rules, it seems fashionable now to call them a sociopath or a narcissist.

It's this kind of retaliation that keeps most people from speaking out against authority, especially in bureaucratic environments like the typical office setting. The threat of repercussions keeps people fearful and submissive. Indeed, in my department, I was always plagued by two opposing forces: Speak up against hypocrisy and injustice and suffer the consequences, or keep my mouth shut and experience a loss of integrity.

Meanwhile, attempting to see myself as having a problem with authority was alienating and wounded my self-esteem. The "bad boy" label didn't ring true for me. I was supposed to be a hero, not an antihero!

It wasn't until the summer that I started to understand my own behavior. That's when I read what journalist Bari Weiss put in her resignation letter to the *New York Times*, describing its toxic work culture. Journalist Andrew Sullivan did the same at *New York* magazine. And so did journalist Glenn Greenwald, who cited illiberalism and censorship at *The Intercept*, which he had co-founded.

Darkly inspired by these independent-minded journalists who felt muzzled and oppressed in similar authoritarian work environments, I began reading works by activists and revolutionaries. Not surprisingly, my study led to author and activist Noam Chomsky, who inspired me with his words. "I think it only makes sense to seek out and identify structures of authority, hierarchy, and domination in every aspect of life, and to challenge them; unless a justification for them can be given, they are illegitimate, and should be dismantled, to increase the scope of human freedom."

Following the breadcrumbs, I then read *Resisting Illegitimate Authority* by clinical psychologist Bruce E. Levine, Ph.D., a self-described antiauthoritarian. Dr. Levine's book helped me understand that I didn't necessarily have a problem with authority. Rather, I had a problem with *illegitimate* authority, with leaders who were incompetent or untrustworthy and who seemed to exist only to preserve existing power structures. Indeed, I had had no difficulty with *legitimate* authority in the past.

For instance, I once worked at a biomedical research institute on a fundraising team led by a Ph.D. in anthropology from Harvard. She was smart, sincere, and highly capable. She created an egalitarian atmosphere within the small team. Together, the team discussed strategy and made hiring decisions. I respected her and followed her instructions. When authority was competent and genuine, I had no issues. It was only when it became oppressive and untrustworthy that I became a "problem."

Jane, Lydia, and her foot soldiers were just the sort of illegitimate authorities who riled me up. In public meetings, they branded themselves democratic and open-minded, yet in their day-to-day operations, they didn't want collaboration—they expected servitude. It was "their way or the highway" with every project. Their directives and requirements were often exploitative, and they exercised their dominance covertly by relying on private meetings or emails to keep employees in line. I also thought Lydia and her team were illegitimate because they were mere coordinators of the creative projects. Most of the time, they instructed creative individuals like me or contracted others from advertising agencies. They rarely did any of the work themselves.

Moreover, while I revered the hospital and the clinicians and scientists who worked there, they were a means to an end for Lydia, Jane, and the marketing folks. This, too, made them illegitimate authorities in my eyes. They looked at healthcare providers and other medical experts as vehicles for brand building and profit. Even less care and sympathy were given to the patients whose lives they exploited for TV and radio ads, marketing articles, and promotional videos. To the marketing team, these patients' maladies—their cancers or heart diseases—represented "high-priority areas." Little attention was paid to the fact that such commodities were living, breathing humans, many of whom were suffering through the worst times of their lives. They were treated as assets in a bizarre game of selling medicine to prospective patients.

Who was I to talk, though? I interviewed patients and doctors and wrote articles and advertisements featuring them. Whenever I saw patients depicted in an article, advertisement, or video I'd written, I was satisfied that I might have helped raise public awareness of a disease or exposed the hospital's services, but I was also troubled. While I had sympathized with the patients I interviewed, how much had I *really* cared about them and their illnesses? Did I just get what I needed for my writing project? Perhaps I disliked Lydia and her team because they were mirrors reflecting back to me the person my job had helped me to become.

This all hit home when I saw a woman I'd once dated appear in a TV commercial for a cancer institute. "I wanted a cancer clinic where I knew I would get the very best care," she said in the ad. Knowing her,

I recognized that "very best care" wasn't part of her vernacular. The line would have been written by someone like me who crafted talking points in advance of on-camera interviews. If subjects didn't mouth marketing messages in their interview, they were asked to read the talking points on camera. More often than not, these canned "responses" were the ones used in a commercial's final cut.

Reading further about antiauthoritarianism, I came to believe that bureaucrats like Norah, Lydia, and Jane felt justified in their controlling behavior because they were usually directed to behave that way by their superiors. Even if the conduct violated their conscience, they could justify it through rationalization: "I'm just doing my job." This attitude is reminiscent of the phenomenon Hannah Arendt refers to as "the banality of evil"—the terrifying apathy that rational individuals can exhibit when they're involved in or witnessing something unjust.

While some might not view corporate politics on the same level as government politics, the indignities I have seen coworkers suffer in the halls of American corporations is shocking. "When you think of the long and gloomy history of man," wrote scientist and novelist C. P. Snow, "you will find that far more, and far more hideous, crimes have been committed in the name of obedience than have ever been committed in the name of rebellion." I have seen many firsthand.

As I continued reading, I realized the marketing team had become a totalitarian system, depriving employees of their dignity, integrity, and humanity. Broadly speaking, the rise in corporate power in the United States and beyond had become disconcerting to me, as corporations essentially enslaved their laborers within hierarchical systems that demanded blind obedience. This was the devastating reality of capitalism, according to Noam Chomsky. "It's ridiculous to talk about freedom in a society dominated by huge corporations. What kind of freedom is there inside a corporation? They're totalitarian institutions—you take orders from above and maybe give them to people below you. There's about as much freedom as under Stalinism."

After two years of working within this oppressive corporate culture, I started to see my identity through a new lens. I wasn't a rebel with anti-authority tendencies. Nor was I suffering from "oppositional defiant disorder," a pathology my father liked to brand me with in childhood whenever I rebelled against his strict parenting style. Rather, like Chomsky, Levine, and the other writers I was reading, I was antiauthoritarian. I challenged and resisted those who acted as illegitimate authorities.

While I felt empowered by my new sense of identity, many of my colleagues seemed to be suffering in silence in the toxic workplace. Their work lacked meaning, and the culture demanded fearful obedience, alienating them from the value of their work products. Was it any wonder our department often lost employees to "better opportunities"? The restructuring had invited in Lydia, Jane, and other authoritarian leaders, who had, in turn, built an oppressive environment. Because no one had the courage to speak up about the working conditions, Lydia, Jane, and others could act with impunity. The people who left the department for new jobs neglected to tell anyone, including HR, the truth. Those who left probably supposed the issues were so pervasive that they couldn't be reformed. Perhaps they just wanted to put the department in their rearview mirrors.

While it was painful to step out from the crowd, I was growing into my role as an antiauthoritarian, learning to embrace the hard work required to "question, challenge, and resist illegitimate authority," as Dr. Levine wrote. After clashing with Jane mostly through emails, I found my anger reaching a fever pitch.

"I'm not happy with Jane's supervision," I told Norah in our quarterly meeting. "And the domineering culture Lydia and her team have created has become toxic."

"I think you should try mediation with Jane," Norah said. "Before that, though, can you write up a summary of your grievances?"

I sent Norah a three-page document stating that my conflict came from the toxic and psychologically unsafe environment created by an authoritarian culture. Norah shared the letter with Lydia, Max, and Jane. Though Norah had assured me my job was secure, I was certain the letter would get me fired, as other openly unhappy employees who had complained had been let go quickly and without explanation, including two highly creative professionals.

To my surprise, things got better for a while. Jane created more manageable deadlines, feedback from her and the marketing team became less critical, and most of the oppression lifted. Norah even reviewed HR's training videos and agreed it didn't make sense for our department to be forced to view them all. Afterward, it took employees half the time to complete them.

These positive developments happened because I spoke up. This was a watershed moment for me. After confronting authoritarian leaders, I hadn't been marginalized, punished, or terminated. I had spoken my mind, and things had improved. This contributed to my sense of self-worth. I had my integrity. An identity, even.

The mediators put me in contact with a career coach in their office. Abigail provided an open, warm, and nonjudgmental space for self-discovery. Together, Abigail and I discovered insights that led me to new and meaningful ways of perceiving myself, which led me to a more positive self-understanding. We considered ways to use my creativity and idealism effectively in corporate environments. I made lists of my values: creativity, adventure, wisdom, freedom, and meaning. I also made a list of people I admired, like Oliver Sacks, Michael Crichton, Rachel Carson, Carl Sagan, Friedrich Nietzsche, Albert Camus, among others. Abigail speculated that perhaps my creative personality and innovative thinking style were clashing with the hierarchical, bureaucratic environment of the organization.

"You'd probably be happier at a company with creative and nonhierarchical organizational structures, like the design consultancy company IDEO."

I agreed and began applying for jobs in creative departments at companies that seemed to welcome new ideas, not roll their eyes at them.

Abigail and I also talked about the virtues of having a day job to support me financially and emotionally while I wrote essays and fiction on the side.

We also discussed how my direct, blunt communication style could sometimes incite or insult people. She suggested using "nonviolent communication" techniques to get my points across. From reading Marshall Rosenberg's *Nonviolent Communication*, I learned I was often accusatorial while trying to resolve a conflict with someone—especially Jane. Instead of telling Jane I wanted to be heard and have my ideas validated—not necessarily implemented, just heard—I asked her to stop talking to me like a robot. Instead of asking her to respect my process and give me realistic amounts of time to develop writing products, I would tell her she was a slave driver and that her deadlines were impractical and unfair.

Being called a robot and a slave driver put Jane on the defensive—and moved me further from my goal of being valued as a creative employee. Instead of expressing how Jane was failing or what I thought was wrong with her and her management style, I began trying to express my feelings and what I needed to be an effective member of the team. I was still far from mastering nonviolent communication, but at least I was making an effort to implement the new communication style.

During our last meeting together, Abigail and I discussed anger, an emotion I felt quite often in my work environment.

"Anger has many underlying sources," she said. "Do you know what's causing your anger when it bubbles to the surface?"

The introspective practice allowed me to get more in touch with my feelings, something not always easy for men of my generation. "If I'm angry at Jane, I'm usually just feeling ignored, disempowered, or humiliated."

Two years after the restructuring, another shake-up was in the works. The system of twelve hospitals to which my hospital belonged had hired a chief marketing officer (CMO), tasked with consolidating all the marketing teams into one centralized department. Predictably, I watched Lydia promote members of her team to senior titles to position them for leadership roles on the new sixty-person team.

In our first video conference with the new CMO, Lydia advertised the content and digital teams as "passionate and curious." The two personality traits had often gotten me into trouble, but they no doubt sounded great to a new boss who probably gorged himself on *Harvard Business Review* articles extolling the virtues of building a team of innovative thinkers. Such curiosity and passion had always been discouraged in the day-to-day; Lydia, Jane, and others just wanted projects finished quickly and according to their demands. Yet here, Lydia was leveraging these qualities because it bolstered her image as a leader. Ever the sycophant, she cozied up to the new CMO and soon grabbed herself an executive position while securing a leadership role for one of her lieutenants.

Not long after, Lydia submitted her resignation, having leveraged the newly minted title to climb higher up the ladder at a new hospital in a different state. A few weeks before leaving, she suddenly fired Max for unknown reasons; some of us speculated that he'd raised concerns about the toxic environment she'd helped create.

At this point, I'd seen enough, and I'd already been through one restructuring with the hospital; another was not on my list of priorities. I started interviewing for new jobs. With insights from Abigail in mind, I avoided applying to companies that likely had rigid corporate environments, perhaps inhabited by authorities who demanded uncritical obedience. Rather, I sought to work in a creative, experimental culture, a place where I could "think different" without feeling like Randle Patrick McMurphy.

Eventually, I was offered a job as a copywriter in the marketing team of a company that designs, develops, and sells audio technology, including speakers, headphones, home theater systems, and professional audio products. The company was founded on values such as creativity, boldness, and innovation. In interviews, the new team was open-minded and humorous, and I got the sense we'd work well together.

Two days before Christmas, I submitted my resignation to Jane. My last day was December 31. That morning, I sent my department a scathing review of the last two years, effectively burning bridges with everyone. The following Monday, a work friend told me that Norah and her old public relations team had split off from the department, effectively burying the truth and leaving the marketing team to fend for themselves with the new CMO and larger marketing group.

Before starting my new job, I took three weeks to rest, recharge, and reflect on what had happened. The hypocrisy, deception, and authoritarianism I'd seen in my department had changed me, radicalized me, temporarily turning me into an antihero. I'd seen injustices and had tried to do something about them. Working with illegitimate authorities like Lydia and Jane had made it easier for me to spot legitimate ones. Experiencing oppression made me want to fight for the powerless and those who suffer. These were skills I now had no matter where I went.

I didn't intend to correct every injustice in the world, and of course, injustices far worse than oppressive working conditions in Corporate America would continue to exist. I simply vowed to speak up when I saw wrongdoing in front of me. I had learned that meaningful change and progress typically don't begin with those in power. According to Chomsky, such change "comes out of struggles from below." If I saw something wrong, I would need to say something, because change would never be initiated by the Lydias and Janes of the world.

In the meantime, I would try to get back to being a hero.

CHAPTER 23

Forest Medicine

It was a warm Sunday morning in June when I arrived at Middlesex Fells Reservation, a state park about fifteen minutes north of Boston. My chosen five-mile trail in the Fells was empty and damp from the morning rain. I had decided to take a "forest bath" during my walk in the woods to dull my nerves and lift my mood.

The practice of forest bathing originated in Japan, where it is called *shinrin-yoku*, which translates as "taking in the forest atmosphere." My reading cited studies dating back to the 1980s, which revealed that trees and plants give off volatile substances or oils called phytoncides. These invisible chemicals have been shown to lower blood pressure and heart rate, boost the immune system, alleviate anxiety by reducing stress hormones, and maybe even fight off depression. It sounded too good to be true. Yet here I was, looking for forest remedies.

The "forest as medicine" concept wasn't foreign to me. I often went to the woods when I needed to refresh. Several years ago, when I had returned from a year-long stay in southern California, I stayed in my father's house in New Hampshire for a few weeks before starting a new job in Boston. Living so far from home in California and surviving off my dwindling savings had produced free-floating anxiety. To adjust the volume on my nervous system, I put myself on a regime of forest baths, hiking a small hill near my father's house every day. At the top, I would soak in the beautiful views of rolling mountains and sometimes meditate in silence.

Having been raised in the White Mountains of New Hampshire, I spent much of my childhood outdoors. When my brother and I weren't in school, my father would kick us out of the house to explore. We would dart through the woods, build forts in trees, wade into streams and wrangle tadpoles in ponds. In summer camp, we paddled across lakes and hiked the majestic mountains of the Presidential Range.

For the last fifteen years, I've been a city dweller, and I've started to feel semi-captive, a condition the naturalist John Muir described as "tired, nerve-shaken, over-civilized." My father, who lives in the sleepy town of Eaton with a population of about 400 people, felt similarly when he graduated from high school in Sudbury, Massachusetts. The summer after he graduated, he went north and settled in Mount Washington Valley to live in the mountains. "If I lived where you lived, I'd be in jail," he once confessed to me when we were deadlocked in Boston traffic. I could relate to the frustration the city seemed to bring out in my father, and I often felt rattled by urban life.

As I walked the footpaths in the Fells, I followed the advice of forest-bathing practitioners. I was supposed to be mindful of my senses as I strolled through the woods. I relished the absence of Boston's clamor—car engines and horns, shrieking sirens, the dull roar of tractor-trailer trucks gearing down. As I walked, I felt the earth beneath my sneakers. I inhaled the scent of the white pines, felt the texture of the breeze, and listened to the symphony of birds and insects around me. Ten minutes into the walk, I paused to look over a pond. The sun warmed my face.

In the middle of Middlesex Fells, I left the dirt path, walked to the edge of a cliff, and looked out over a tranquil lake. The wind blew the scent of hemlock trees into my face. I knew that I'd return to a small apartment in Boston in a few hours and a cramped office space the next morning, but the woods would always be available to me when I needed to refresh. A dog strolled up beside me, closed its eyes, and lifted its nose into the air. I, too, closed my eyes and inhaled the forest's medicine.

CHAPTER 24

The Language of My Father

Several years ago, my father and two of his friends got lost during a long motorcycle ride in Mexico. When his friends stopped to study maps of the area, my father made a gut decision and led them down an unknown road. His instinct turned out to be wrong, and they ended up backtracking. According to my father's friends, on motorcycle trips like this one, he is mistaken about nine times out of ten.

In matters of navigation, my father likes to believe he has a superior sense of direction because he's part Native American. Given this claim of heritage—for which there is little evidence—and the fact that his gut decisions during motorcycle rides are often wrong, his friends nicknamed him Tonto, after the fictional Native American companion in the TV show *The Lone Ranger*. In Spanish, *tonto* means "fool."

As a general contractor in a small New England town, my father has spent the last three decades as a self-employed contractor—doing every kind of construction project: from roofs to interior renovations, from single-room remodels to full houses. In the last few years, he's found a niche in building custom homes. The process involves working with an architect to design a house, build it on land he's bought, and then find buyers with his veteran realtor. It's called speculative housebuilding because the project is carried out before a buyer is found. It's a risky business, especially in an uncertain economy, but my father has done it several times and plans to do more.

After my father has built a home on spec, prospective buyers can contact his realtor, who puts them in contact with my father. My father is quick to arrange a meeting with the clients at the house—oftentimes on the same day, sometimes within the same hour. The 64-year-old builder displays adept conversational skills when meeting with clients. No one would call him eloquent, but he's well-spoken. He's polite, listens attentively, and responds respectfully. No hard sell. He charms without trying, giving off an air of nonchalance. And when the economy is strong, people buy his spec houses.

At one point, however, a deal fell through after a client had "lost faith" in him. Trying to understand what might've happened, I asked my father to tell me the story. It wasn't until we dissected his written communications that I realized what had caused the deal to fail. The emails he had sent weren't just poorly written; they were incomprehensible.

To illustrate my father's written style, here's an email he sent to a friend, in which he discusses where they could potentially find land to buy.

> doesn't matter 2 much.what about water.what about that place over by the squam lake.by the birdie place.it overhangs the water.has a bowling alley.it;s near the foreign car place.113 and 3 mayb toward ashland

To read an email from my father is to read a long string of symbols barely recognizable as letters, words, and sentences. As you can see, the prose is a series of thoughts jumbled into disjointed sentence fragments. It uses incorrect punctuation and grammar, and misspellings are rampant. Few breaks are provided by commas or spacing after periods. In short, my father's emails are gobbledygook.

After receiving emails such as these, the same friends who nicknamed my father Tonto coined a name for his writing style: Tontonese. The language of Tontonese lacks due diligence. When an important thought enters my father's brain, he grabs his laptop or phone, types within an email until he's exhausted the thought, and presses send. He doesn't double-check to make sure what he's written is comprehensible. He doesn't edit or proofread. He thinks it, types it, and fires it off.

One might think that writing emails in Tontonese is a benign quirk, the somewhat amusing trait of a baby boomer with anti-technology tendencies. But this language has serious consequences in business dealings. On the job site, clients meet a friendly, sociable man, yet his emails look like they're written by a kindergartener. Tontonese strains his credibility. The clients my father charms in person question his intelligence, not to mention his construction skills, after receiving his indecipherable emails.

In the following email, my father writes to his friend about mountain biking. What he's trying to get at, though, is anyone's guess.

The Language of My Father

i got there they had left.i was there at 10 till 6.John said it was 5:30. talk 2 him about his bike.we could meet him.i am going 2 try and slip a ride in this afternoon.tc may go.time will depend on the Jackson folks.haven't heard bak from them.i e mailed them yesterday aft.i ride a santa cruz blur carbon.my last bike was a blur lt.they are a smoking bike.do u no of 1 for sale?i will bring my puta.i may have time 2 ck today

After some reflection, I realized the first major problem with Tontonese is that there's no Rosetta Stone for this language, so clients, friends, and family who receive my father's messages often can't understand his point. The biggest issue, however, is that my father's friendly nature—his charm, his *humanity*—are lost in translation.

This was all the more frustrating because, as a full-time copywriter, my emails are well-crafted and almost always error-free. With a decade of experience, I've developed a kind of meta-consciousness, where everything I write is simultaneously evaluated through the lens of my imagined reader: Is that sentence clear? Do I need more or less? Do I even *need* that sentence? Before sending any written communication, I check it several times. Call me neurotic, but I want to communicate clearly. A reader has to decipher tiny symbols on a screen or page; I want to make their job as easy as possible. Right or wrong, I think that using language to communicate effectively reflects on intelligence and thoughtfulness, and I wish to make a favorable impression. And yes, I care about language and cringe when I see my father treating it with the same delicacy a lion uses when it's devouring its lunch.

I decided to stage an intervention, thinking I might prevent future business dealings from falling through. I recommended that my father stop emailing clients and conduct all his business dealings where he flourishes: in person or over the phone. One language dies out every fourteen days, according to *National Geographic* magazine; I told my father that Tontonese must go extinct.

Alas, my words fell on deaf ears, and he continued writing emails in Tontonese. He told me that dashing off an email in his preferred language saves time compared to picking up the phone or arranging an in-person meeting. If a job requires an excavator and my father knows one who could start the next morning, why not quickly relay that through an email? And why fancy up the language with periods and commas when sentence fragments should get his message across? My father's been self-employed for thirty years, with enough demand to cover his expenses and keep food on the table. If a client doesn't want him to build their home because of his emails? "Who cares," he likes to say. And, without further thought, he moves on.

Eventually, I stopped hassling my father about his emails, because I accepted that he'll never take the time to learn even the most basic tenets of grammar. I doubt he'll read through an email before hitting send. While often bewildered, most people who receive my father's emails eventually accept that Tontonese doesn't reflect his intelligence or his competence as a builder. Self-employed and often busy, he's just more interested in building than spending time talking about building. For better or worse, Tontonese is his mother tongue. And while he may be Tonto, my father is no fool.

CHAPTER 25

Learning to Love My Fate

For more than a decade, I've worked as a writer for American organizations. I'm good at the work and have found a niche. But I have increasingly started to feel as though I am little more than a propagandist for businesses and nonprofits. In these jobs, where I often work within marketing departments, nothing I write is entirely truthful. Rather, everything is crafted and spun to promote a service, product, or brand.

For example, my writing for a hospital often involves interviewing patients and writing articles to "tell their stories." After I develop an article about a patient's experience, a team of marketers weighs in on my draft to edit, spin, and sterilize it in order to project the best possible image of the hospital. While the team's edits don't inject overt lies into the stories, they do omit any potentially negative aspects. As such, the published stories are based on real events but are far from genuine depictions.

During the Coronavirus Pandemic, I wrote many patient stories and articles designed to portray the hospital as safe to visit. These "don't delay your care" stories were sophisticated attempts to influence the behavior of consumers seeking medical care. It was true that the hospital had been vigilant in implementing safety measures to limit the spread of the virus and safeguard both patients and staff. Therefore, I could do the work and sleep at night.

Still, I was becoming discontent with writing marketing copy. I also had the sense that people were picking up on my cognitive dissonance. In the past four years, two employers have offered me new copywriting positions with more responsibility and higher salaries, but I turned them down because of my growing dissatisfaction with a copywriting career. A year later, I interviewed for two more jobs, but came in second each time. Was my evolving self-image obvious to employers? They likely saw that I could fulfill the duties of the job, but could they also see that I thought of myself as a corporate hack? Perhaps they sensed I was conflicted about my place in the world and might be uncomfortable churning out sales material. Why would an employer hire someone with such a "bad attitude"?

In high school and college, I wanted to become a doctor. Scoring poorly on the entrance exam for medical school, I pivoted to graduate school in order to become a scientist. When I realized that the traditional scientific path wasn't for me, I committed myself to writing about science—but never once did I envision myself as someone who would spin science and medicine for profit. Whenever someone learns that I work in marketing, I feel ashamed.

Nevertheless, I've been employed in marketing departments for most of my thirties, among people whose values I don't share. Many of my coworkers majored in marketing in college, and most of them have spent time in advertising agencies. Proficient bureaucrats, they constantly jockey for advancement and scheme for power, always preoccupied with self-preservation. Because they scrutinize everything I write, I'm at the mercy of people I'm not particularly fond of.

My disenchantment with writing marketing copy grew in my early thirties as I began to write more essays and fiction. At 35, I enrolled in an MFA program in creative writing. There I wrote my third novel, several short stories, and a handful of essays. During our program's ten-day writing residencies, I spent time with other writers who were passionate about writing and storytelling, and it was thrilling to compare notes. Following my growing interest in the arts and humanities, I read biographies and watched documentaries about artists and writers I admired. As I read and watched, I tried to comprehend how they had mastered their crafts and gained prominence. Increasingly, all I wanted was to spend my time creating art, just like the people I was studying.

I also came to admire journalists, especially independent journalists like Bari Weiss, Matt Taibbi, and Glenn Greenwald, who aren't afraid to speak truth to power. I'm inspired by movies like *Spotlight*, *State of Play*, and *All the President's Men*, which depict reporters "comforting the afflicted and afflicting the comfortable" and prove that journalists make a difference in the world. I never miss *60 Minutes* and find journalists like

Bob Whittaker and Lesley Stahl to be true heroes, taking on major issues for the benefit of the public.

I sometimes fantasize about writing for a newspaper or magazine full-time, but whenever I apply for a journalism job, I get no response. I've wondered if the Fourth Estate looks at marketing writers like me with suspicion. Perhaps I'm too subjective, too personal, or too imaginative for traditional journalism.

Over the years, my admiration has grown for creative writers with an activist spirit. One such writer is Rachel Carson, the author of *Silent Spring*, a book that sounded the alarm on pesticides and sparked an environmental movement in the 1960s. After poring over studies about the effects of dichloro-diphenyl-trichloroethane (DDT) on wildlife and the environment, Carson said, "What I discovered was that everything which meant most to me as a naturalist was being threatened, and that nothing I could do would be more important."

Carson went to work in a time of great need, as all artists must do. Scientists had known about the problem of harmful chemicals, and the public had its suspicions, but it took an artist like her to change minds by turning scientific complexity into lyrical prose. Carson pioneered a novel way of writing about science that cut through the statistics and figures. She made people not only think but feel.

As a writer of marketing material, my affection for Carson likely comes from the fact that her work is unbiased and pure, a far cry from the selling and spinning I do on a daily basis. Perhaps I admire journalists like Weiss, Taibbi, and Greenwald because they also write about subjects that matter. In my role as a hired gun for corporations, I often wonder whether the web pages, marketing articles, and promotional videos I develop are adding up to anything at all. Do people even read the stuff we dump onto the Internet? Does this content matter? What good does my work in my day job do in the world?

As I find myself called to a more artistic path, I've started to see my corporate work for what it is: a day job. As I continue to write essays and fiction in my spare time, I've started to clearly see how difficult it is to flourish in the world as an artist. It's not until you devote yourself to creative work that you realize how much life seems designed to knock you down at every stage of your development. Even though the artist plays a vital role in society—as a social conscience who often interprets reality and writes about how (and often why) to live—many individuals are intolerant of the artist's flights of fancy. Most people are practical and have better things to do than entertain the artist's idealism and unrealistic vision of the future. Most adults seem to want to gain enough money to keep themselves and their families healthy, maybe to catch a movie or a ballgame or host a barbeque. Most can't seem to fathom why anyone hasn't figured out their life by their thirties. Indeed, it's often embarrassing to admit that I'm still struggling to find my place in the world.

A young artist also learns that making art, especially in the early stages, isn't a path to riches. One needs money to pay rent and buy food; hence developing artists live in limbo between the practical world of commerce and the dreamy, sometimes subversive spaces where they produce their work. Young artists must play the game. They contribute to the world's affairs while working a day job that exploits their talents for profit. The artist might long to be free, but he must rely on the capitalistic machine for financial security, perhaps wounding his dignity in the process.

If society is set up this way, why not leave the workforce and live cheaply while writing essays and fiction? I tried that for a year and ran out of money, realizing that a day job supports me in growing and learning my craft. Plus, moving to a cabin in the woods to live the life of a "true artist" may not be the solution to my existential dilemmas. First of all, a day job, it turns out, provides grist for the mill. The "real world" is a mess, but it can be a big, beautiful mess and can often be the source of stories. Moreover, while it can sometimes be disheartening to work in the corporate machine, it can also be thrilling to be part of this world and its everyday affairs. In the modern-day office, I occasionally feel like an actor on the world's stage, playing a small part in the grand theater of life.

Though it might sound counterintuitive, I sometimes feel drawn to the absurdity of bureaucratic systems, which I can challenge and try to fix. In my current day job, I'm in the big, beautiful mess, solving business problems. Rather than developing theories in the halls of academia, I prefer to apply philosophical concepts to real-world problems. Every once in a while, I even find myself trying to elevate the banal conversations around the office by sometimes asking "big questions" in the most palatable way: through humor. In the office kitchen, there's nothing quite as amusing as dryly asking a question like, "Why do so many of us die without ever learning how to live?" while your coworker adds half-and-half to their coffee.

There's also something comforting about being anchored to the hustle and bustle of civilization through a day job. When I was freelancing for a year and mostly living off savings, I felt unmoored from the happenings of the world. I was following my dreams to write creative nonfiction and fiction, but I was a man without a cause, and I spun out because of it. I often wonder if that's why the philosopher Friedrich Nietzsche descended into madness toward the end of his life, much of which he spent as a nomadic explorer of the human condition in place of the teaching post he'd had for several years.

While a day job can sometimes be a hard pill to swallow, it can provide a ready-made purpose each day that helps keep my feet on the ground as I navigate my uncertain creative life. Perhaps most importantly, a day job also provides the budding artist with security, freeing the mind from worry over money. Feeling safe and secure—as much as one can in a human life—fuels writing projects. I've found that I can't create art if I'm fretting over my checking account. During the year that I wasn't working a traditional nine-to-five job, I didn't write a word of fiction. Instead, I wrote articles and marketing copy—stuff that pays (though not much).

Furthermore, being productive and creative in my staff writing job often breeds inspiration and efficiency in my creative writing. I have many examples of times when I fictionalized circumstances from my job.

Why am I so ungrateful toward corporations? Most of my employers have supported my career development. They've mentored me, paid for me to attend conferences and workshops, and bought me meals while traveling. Moreover, without the money from my salary, I wouldn't be able to move my creative projects forward. I reinvest a lot of my money into hiring editors, designers, illustrators, videographers, website developers, even writers. The salaries from my day jobs have given me the freedom to be creative on the side.

Why do I perceive working for corporations as an exploitation of my skills? Why can't I see it as my duty as a citizen? In his book *Meditations*, the Roman emperor Marcus Aurelius said that he got himself out of bed each day by reminding himself that many people were relying on him. It was his *duty* to show up for work. Couldn't I look at my day job similarly? Why not make some commercial art by day while writing essays and fiction on the side? It's a rather privileged position in society: Many people would love a full-time writing job like mine. Perhaps I should try to be grateful for what I have instead of criticizing my place in the world and always striving for more.

Moreover, if I can maintain a high level of production in my creative life while holding down a corporate job, am I already doing what I should be doing? Do I already have what I want? Have I already arrived, so to speak? Then again, how many commercial writers like me toil away at day jobs and never break through with their more artistic work? Is this a matter of talent or luck? Or do some people give up too soon? For me, writing is a compulsion, an activity that I find immensely challenging yet rewarding. It is something that gives my life meaning. But how long does it take to break through, and am I willing to wait as long as it takes?

For me, the answer to the latter is yes, but I suppose every evolving artist wonders if it will ever happen for them. Much ink has been spilled about the famous 10,000 hours a person supposedly needs to accumulate to master any given skill. Having started writing seriously in my late twenties, I'm surely close to that mark. Is a breakthrough imminent, or does it differ for each person, as I suspect it does?

I suppose that most creative people never think that their time comes quickly enough. When I got my first copywriting job a decade ago, hoping that the position would help make me become a better writer, I thought I might leave the workforce and write full-time after the publication of my first novel. I thought wrong. Having self-published two novels, and published my third with a hybrid publisher, I know that achieving our dreams doesn't happen as fast as we'd like.

I've found some comfort in reading about the lives of other writers who held down day jobs to support their creative work. Many writers wrote advertising copy before their creative writing took off: F. Scott Fitzgerald, Dr. Seuss, and James Patterson come to mind. John Grisham worked as a lawyer for years while he wrote legal thrillers at night. Sam Shem, author of the satirical novel *House of God*, went to medical school knowing that practicing medicine would be his day job. He wanted to be a writer, but he didn't want to have to make money from it. Medicine paid the bills.

Author and neurologist Oliver Sacks found a similar dynamic in his life. In fact, some of Sacks's most fascinating patients became published case studies, which he crafted to read like fiction. A recent documentary about Sacks described him as a writer who "storied" people into the world. Had he retreated to a cabin in the woods to write what he wanted, the world might not have benefited from his observations about the brain and mind and their malfunctions.

Even so, this idea of moving to a cabin in the woods is a romantic notion among those with artistic sensibilities. It captured the imagination of Henry David Thoreau. When he decided to become a writer, he first moved to where all the great writers were—New York City. But he failed to thrive there. A rugged individualist and a bit rough around the edges, Thoreau wasn't accepted into the city's literary society, so he went back to Concord, Massachusetts, where he had lived and grown up. Not long after, he began his great experiment in living at Walden Pond.

So what path am I on? I don't think it's the path of the scholar, the educator, or even the journalist. It's the path of the artist, and the discontent and confusion I feel come from the fact that there is no set path for the artist. The creative life is one of always making it up as you go. As I work on one creative project after another, it's tempting to reach for a metaphor that depicts life as an endless struggle without meaning. I could imagine myself like Sisyphus, who was forced to endlessly roll a boulder up a mountain, only to watch it fall to the base. Could I, as Albert Camus did in "The Myth of Sisyphus," imagine Sisyphus as happy in the absurdity of his situation? Perhaps, but that's not the metaphor I want to choose for myself. It doesn't accept the fact that despite my best efforts to roll those boulders happily, I will always be trying to take control.

Instead, the metaphor I choose to guide my life, for now, is the notion of "loving one's fate," as Nietzsche put it—to know that everything that's happened in my life has contributed to who I am and what I'm doing in this moment, to know that I'm both limited by my circumstances and also free to pursue any project I find meaningful. I'm both restricted by my circumstances and free to try to transcend them. This is the compromise of living a human life.

What if I never write my way out of corporate work? What if I always need a day job? These outcomes may not be entirely within my control. Maybe my proverbial cabin is coming. Maybe I just need to gather more experience before I leave the workforce for good. But maybe not. Only time will tell. Indeed, these questions might not even matter. For now, I accept where I am, who I am, and what I have found myself doing at this time of my life. I will try as best I can to love my fate, because as Nietzsche said, it is my life.

Epilogue

At the end of 2020, I resigned from my writing position in the marketing department of a major hospital in Boston. The work environment created by authoritarian leadership had simply become too toxic. Unbeknownst to management, I had spent the previous two years observing and recording their mistreatment of people.

By the time I got a new job as a copywriter for an audio technology company in January 2021, I had begun working on "Corporate Disobedience," an essay exploring everything I'd witnessed in that marketing department. The story took me months to write and more than two years to publish.

A week before I started my new job, the Capitol riots of January 6 left me frightened by the powerful influence of propaganda and misinformation on the hearts and minds of the public. That same week, I stumbled over *How to Start a Revolution*, a documentary about the political theorist Gene Sharp. He studied and wrote about nonviolent resistance, and his ideas and analyses helped promote democracy movements all over the world. He'd founded the Albert Einstein Institution (AEI) based in Boston.

The day after watching *How to Start a Revolution*, I emailed the institution's executive director, asking if she'd be open to talking. She agreed, and we had a productive discussion about nonviolent resistance and the institution's ongoing work to create educational training for activists interested in using the principles Gene Sharp pioneered in their freedom movements worldwide.

Over the next two years, I wrote copy for the audio company and helped develop advertising campaigns to launch several consumer electronics products. Meanwhile, I kept in touch with AEI's executive director, editing written materials on a volunteer basis, and continued reading about nonviolent resistance and civil disobedience.

In my spare time, I worked on "Corporate Disobedience," using the essay to better understand myself and where I wanted to be in the world. I came to realize I had always been a rebel, dating back to my childhood, during which I rebelled against my father's semi-authoritarian parenting style and strict control of the household.

Did it not make sense, then, that I would chafe within corporate environments, where people are trapped in hierarchies, not allowed to think for themselves? Was it any surprise I was often branded as a troublemaker in such environments? I was independently-minded and resistant to the groupthink or cult-like forces that influenced workers in corporate settings.

Despite enjoying the creative challenges at the audio company, I became disengaged in my role. As a copywriter, I felt like my creative writing abilities were being exploited to sell consumer electronics. To anyone who would listen, I confessed to being nothing more than a propagandist, a useful idiot in the advertising industry.

Inspired by Gene Sharp's writings and the mission of the institution he established, I started following groups that supported human rights and strategic nonviolent resistance. In the fall of 2022, I jumped at the opportunity to attend the Oslo Freedom Forum in New York City.

As I sat in the audience at the conference listening to an activist deliver a passionate speech on human rights, I wondered if the executive director of Gene Sharp's institution was in attendance. Pulling out my phone, I sent her an email asking if she was, to which she replied in the affirmative. We met after the conference to catch up, and I sensed she needed support in her duties, especially with regard to communications.

Not long after, I took a week off work and developed a presentation recommending branding strategies for the institution and a model for staffing a small communications department. I even wrote a job description for a senior communications manager role. I presented the ideas to the executive director at a coffee shop in Boston's South End. It was a productive meeting, and she liked the ideas, but we parted ways without much of a plan for following up.

As winter came, I grew more discontent in my job. There had been layoffs that year and massive changes within the company that had left everyone weary and on edge. Meanwhile, managers were informing the creative department of how much money the company had made because of our holiday advertising campaigns. While consumer electronics like

Epilogue

portable speakers and earbuds could enrich people's lives in many ways, I didn't feel like I was making any real difference in the world.

I applied for several jobs in industries I thought I would be happier in. I was in the second round of interviews for one when I got an email from the executive director of the Albert Einstein Institution saying she'd like to talk about my joining the institution. I didn't know what she had in mind, but I was excited about the prospect of working for the nonprofit organization.

The day we met, I learned I didn't get the job for which I had been interviewing, but the executive director offered me a job to manage the institution's communications. I'd spent two years building a relationship with this person, preparing for a role like the one she offered me. It didn't take me long to accept her offer.

In February 2023, on my last day at the audio company and two weeks before my start date at the institution, "Corporate Disobedience" was published in the *Journal of Autoethnography*. The essay explored how I'd found a new identity as an antiauthoritarian—someone who resists illegitimate authorities—and an advocate for freedom. In my current role at AEI, I help disseminate educational resources to people around the world who need insights and tactics to fight back against oppressive conditions through strategic nonviolent action.

The somewhat serendipitous forces that led me to this work made me think about the amount of control we have over the course of our lives. Are our lives the result of random forces, or are they predetermined based on who we are? Perhaps it's a little bit of both, as Forrest Gump believed by the end of the movie: Random forces are always shaping us, but we, in turn, can shape those forces through the choices we make. Ultimately, the major theme of this essay collection is the question of how much freedom we really have over the direction of our lives.

In Part I of this book, I explored Søren Kierkegaard's idea of the dizziness of freedom in an essay of the same name. I've come to believe that part of the task of living a meaningful life is to place limitations on our own freedom not only through choices of career, family, and relationships but also in how we manage our days, months, and years. Everyone needs a certain amount of freedom to flourish in life, but if you give yourself too much freedom, your life can sprawl and you can flounder.

Freedom, it seems to me, has a sweet spot. To avoid the "dizzying" effects of freedom, we must impose limitations on ourselves through structure and routine, perhaps even monotony. These constraints are unique to everyone. While I can't know the random forces that will act upon me in the future, I can make choices today in hopes of hitting that sweet spot of freedom and giving myself just the right amount of self-discipline to live the life I want to live.

Publication History

These essays were originally published as follows:

"Personal Journey: A Sudden Stab of Murky Suspicion," *The Philadelphia Inquirer*, 2014
"My Terrifying Kilimanjaro Climb: How I Expanded my Limits, but Almost Lost my Mind," *Salon*, 2015
"The Dizziness of Freedom," *The Expeditioner*, 2014
"A Taste of Glory," *Narratively*, 2014
"Bikin' with Thoreau in Mind," *The Boston Globe*, 2016
"Missing Paris," *The Expeditioner*, 2015
"The Hate Game," *The Good Men Project*, 2016
"Departing Down the Middle," *Living Now Magazine*, 2015
"In Beijing It Takes Two Traditional Doctors for One Night's Sleep," *TravelMag*, 2016
"Backed up in China," *Lost Magazine*, 2018
"Walkabout Love in China," *Perceptive Travel*, 2017
"Letters from Dad," *Living Now Magazine*, 2017
"Hoedown at McDonald's," *The Good Men Project*, 2019
"How Do You Woo Someone When You're Still Figuring Out Life?" *The Washington Post*, 2016
"Keeping the Channel Open," *The Good Men Project*, 2019
"Fake It 'til You Make It," *The Manifest-Station*, 2023
"The Gift of Pain," *The Doctor T. J. Eckleburg Review*, 2021
"Sunrise Earth Delivers a Morning Dose of Awe," *The Good Men Project*, 2019
"The Stick," *Drunk Monkeys*, 2022
"How to Fix a Bluey Heart," *The Manifest-Station*, 2021
"Corporate Disobedience," *The Journal of Autoethnography*, 2023
"A Bath in the Forest," *Wanderlust: A Travel Journal*, 2021
"The Language of My Father," *The Atherton Review*, 2022
"Learning to Love My Fate," *Quest: Journal of the Theosophical Society in America*, 2021

www.ingramcontent.com/pod-product-compliance
Ingram Content Group UK Ltd.
Pitfield, Milton Keynes, MK11 3LW, UK
UKHW021834140426
5217IPUK00021B/1435